Grit & Grace

Grit & Grace

UNCOMMON WISDOM FOR INSPIRING LEADERS
DESIGNED TO MAKE YOU THINK

Quotabelle®

ROCK
POINT

Brimming with creative inspiration, how-to projects, and useful information to enrich your everyday life, Quarto Knows is a favorite destination for those pursuing their interests and passions. Visit our site and dig deeper with our books into your area of interest: Quarto Creates, Quarto Cooks, Quarto Homes, Quarto Lives, Quarto Drives, Quarto Explores, Quarto Gifts, or Quarto Kids.

First published in 2018 by Rock Point,
an imprint of The Quarto Group
142 West 36th Street, 4th Floor
New York, NY 10018 USA
T (212) 779-4972 **F** (212) 779-6058
www.QuartoKnows.com

We respect the rights of the people and organizations behind original thinking. It's why we go to great lengths to fact check and give credit where credit is due. Quotes are often considered fair use, and many of the selections in this book are in the public domain. We took an added step to proactively seek permissions for contemporary quotations. And we diligently worked to ensure this collection reflects diversity—of ideas, beliefs, era, culture, geography, career paths, partnering choices, and so on. A sincere thanks to the people who said "yes!"

Rock Point titles are also available at discount for retail, wholesale, promotional, and bulk purchase. For details, contact the Special Sales Manager by email at specialsales@quarto.com or by mail at The Quarto Group, Attn: Special Sales Manager, 401 Second Avenue North, Suite 310, Minneapolis, MN 55401, USA.

10 9 8 7 6 5 4 3 2 1

ISBN: 978-1-63106-530-9

Quotabelle: Pauline Weger and Alicia Williamson
Editorial Director: Rage Kindelsperger
Managing Editor: Erin Canning
Associate Editor: Keyla Hernández
Cover design: Philip Buchanan
Interior design: Merideth Harte

MIX
Paper from
responsible sources
FSC® C104723

Printed in China

CONTENTS

The Quoteur List. 6

New World. New Rules. New Routes. 10

Grit & Grace. 13

Purpose & Chance 27

Heart & Mind 41

Confident & Humble. 55

Community & Self. 69

Wander & Wonder 83

Imagine & Do. 97

Tradition & Innovation 111

Training & Instinct. 125

Courage & Caution 139

Overcome & Become. 153

Conviction & Compromise 167

Speak Up & Listen 181

Substance & Style 195

Get It Done & Unplug. 209

Source It! 222

Please & Thank You 229

About the Authors 232

THE QUOTEUR LIST

quoteur™ / KWŌ TƏR / noun
A person who originates a collection of words worth sharing

Jane Addams 210	Tammy Duckworth 160
Amani Al-Khatahtbeh 190	Milka Duno 106
Madeleine Albright 184	Ava DuVernay 202
Tenley Albright 20	Queen Elizabeth II 227
Marian Anderson 182	Fannie Farmer 112
Susan B. Anthony 168	Tina Fey 134
Courtney Banghart 136	Christiana Figueres 172
Mary Barra 118	Natalie Franke 80
Clara Barton 140	Tulsi Gabbard 176
Erin Benzakein 220	Leymah Gbowee 150
Isabella Bird 84	Elizabeth Gilbert 216
Jeni Britton Bauer 104	Drew Gilpin Faust 170
Tarana Burke 162	Jane Goodall 44
Susan Cain 186	Katharine Graham 16
Minerva Carcaño 58	Mirga Gražinytė-Tyla 192
Judaline Cassidy 60	Alice Greenwald 156
Cher 72	Kelly Holmes 76
Amal Clooney 204	Ayanna Howard 122
Bessie Coleman 142	Dolores Huerta 70
Beth Cross 102	Jessica Jackley 78
Marie Curie 14	Corita Kent 42
Elizabeth Cutler 50	Sue Monk Kidd 32
Sandra Day O'Connor 198	Sung-Joo Kim 34
Ellen DeGeneres 158	Coretta Scott King 18

Wendy Kopp 120

Sallie Krawcheck 148

Cathy Lanier 132

Jennifer Lawrence 178

Maya Lin 146

Lisa Lutoff-Perlo 92

Rose Marcario 22

Meghan Markle 24

Kate McCue 94

Hattie McDaniel 56

Margaret Mead 144

Debbie Millman 36

Maria Montessori 126

Naomi Shihab Nye 90

Maria Popova 52

Beatrix Potter 98

Condoleezza Rice 100

Chita Rivera 88

Robin Roberts 48

Anita Roddick 46

Vera Rubin 86

Maya Rudolph 218

Eunice Kennedy Shriver 30

Anne-Marie Slaughter 214

Megan Smith 74

Muriel Strode 234

Kathryn Sullivan 130

Taylor Swift 164

Junko Tabei 212

Maria Tallchief 128

Dana Tanamachi 64

Alice Paul Tapper 9

Mikaila Ulmer 108

Diana Vreeland 196

Alice Walker 230

Vera Wang 116

Alice Waters 200

Kinari Webb 188

Danielle Weisberg 66

Sheila Wellington 154

Matika Wilbur 206

Venus Williams 174

Reese Witherspoon 62

Susan Wojcicki 38

Tu Youyou 114

Babe Didrikson Zaharias 28

Carly Zakin 66

Dedicated to emerging voices.

(We hear you!)

"Raise your hand."

ALICE PAUL TAPPER

STUDENT • TEN-YEAR-OLD *NEW YORK TIMES* EDITORIALIST •
INSPIRATION FOR A GIRL SCOUT BADGE

New world. New rules. New routes.

TO BUILD THE WORLD YOU IMAGINE YOU CAN'T GO AT IT ALONE.
YOU'RE DESTINED TO MAKE A DIFFERENCE.
ALONG THE WAY, PEOPLE WILL JOIN YOU. MENTORS WILL GUIDE YOU.
AND YOUR OWN STYLE FOR LEADING WILL BEGIN TO TAKE SHAPE.

This book is a personal inspiration gallery, curated especially for modern leaders. We've gathered the ideas and stories of ninety remarkable females—a mix of visible and not so widely known women & girls, from history through today. You'll find artists & athletes, coaches & community builders, entrepreneurs & engineers, scientists & tech titans. Fueled by purpose and lit by passion, these people have inspired those around them to make the world sweeter, greener, fairer, finer, more creative, conscious, connected & streamlined.

What's "uncommon" about them? Their trailblazing careers. Their unexpected life paths. Their unique experiences. Their insights. Ultimately, their impact.

Through research, we discovered that less than 15 percent of the quotations shared every day are from women and girls. In fact, of the 19,800 quotes in one of the most respected quotation resource books, 12 percent were attributed to anonymous authors and only 5 percent to female authors. Missing, too, were ideas by women associated with innovation, science, sports, technology, adventure, art, leadership, and more.

Quotes are pocket wisdom. They're packed with the power to spark an idea, create a connection or light a fire that keeps a team moving forward.

Our aim is to fix the quote supply problem. We're adding missing voices back into history, and creating entrées to a host of true stories. It's how we ensure today's thinkers and doers aren't overlooked going forward.

In *Grit & Grace*, we're going beyond the vaults of familiar, age-old wisdom to scout fresh, real-world advice. We've gathered a collection of ideas lifted from the "aha" moments of intrepid leaders and dished up with intriguing backstories to give you a peek at the hows and whys. There are no rules here. So, take away what speaks to you, adding to your creative toolbox as you craft your own mantra and leadership approach.

The ampersand . . . it's intentional. You may be surprised to learn about its ancient origin as a slapdash shorthand used by Roman scribes. Found in graffiti on walls and hand-lettered on papyrus, those who study language believe the ampersand came from 1st-century writers hastily scribbling "et," which meant "and," often, connecting the two letters to form one.

Over time, the stylized single character came to distinctly stand for "and," even becoming the twenty-seventh letter in the English alphabet at one point. For us, this fascinating figure is a symbol of connection and the importance of dual effort. It's our visual reminder that balance is key to navigating the uncharted paths towards achieving goals big & small. Like the wisdom in *Grit & Grace*, we love that it makes a statement, and that there's a story behind it.

Our hope is that you'll find muses to inspire you as you fashion your own style of leading, and that you'll share what you're loving. After all, leadership is about bringing people along on your journey.

Cheers!
Pauline & Alicia

Grit & Grace

Marie Curie

1867–1934

CHEMIST • FIRST FEMALE NOBEL LAUREATE & FIRST PERSON TO WIN TWO NOBEL PRIZES • MOTHER OF MODERN PHYSICS

When Marie Curie found out she had cancer, she responded with the characteristic calm of a scientist who had dedicated her career to understanding one of nature's most potentially powerful yet dangerous phenomenon: radioactivity. Her diagnosis was just one more occasion to muster courage in a life defined by the unwavering pursuit of knowledge.

As a girl in occupied Poland, Marie's educational opportunities were limited. She worked as a governess to fund her and her sister's studies in Paris. There, she met her husband Pierre. The two scientific devotees bonded over magnetism and became tireless collaborators until Pierre's sudden and tragic death. The first woman to earn a PhD in France, Marie's research at the prestigious Sorbonne University was deemed the "greatest contribution to science" of any thesis project. After her first Nobel win, she eventually became the university's first female professor and lab head. By the time she hung up her lab coat, Marie had expanded the chemical periodic table by two elements (Polonium + Radium) and pioneered the study of radioactivity (a term she coined). Her work influenced everything from x-rays to cancer treatments to carbon dating. She also inspired one of her two daughters to become a Nobel-winning chemist herself!

"Nothing in life is to be feared, it is only to be understood."

MARIE CURIE
SCIENTIST

Katharine Graham

1917–2001

SOCIALITE • FIRST FEMALE FORTUNE 500 CEO •
COURAGEOUS PROTECTOR OF FIRST AMENDMENT RIGHTS

Becoming a leading publisher was not the sort of "fun" Katharine Graham imagined for herself. Her father, owner of the fledgling paper, *The Washington Post,* tapped Katharine's charismatic and savvy husband, Phil, as heir apparent. Phil made great progress, but battled depression, ultimately taking his own life in 1963. Katharine, a middle-aged mother of four, faced a fateful decision: sell the family business or step up to the plate. With no formal business experience, she took a leap of faith. Supported by male mentors, she emerged as one of America's most influential media moguls.

The Washington Post thrived. The company went public during her two decades of leadership. Her paper earned a reputation for stellar journalism, taking risks to release The Pentagon Papers and uncover the Watergate Scandal. When the government tried to suppress her, she took them all the way to the Supreme Court, securing a victory for freedom of the press. Briefly a newsroom journalist herself, Katherine returned to writing to publish a memoir. The book offered a candid account of her rise to power at a moment when the women's movement was only beginning to make waves. It also nabbed her a Pulitzer.

"To love what you do
and feel that it matters—
how could anything
be more fun?"

KATHARINE GRAHAM
PUBLISHER

Coretta Scott King

1927–2006

CONSERVATORY-TRAINED SINGER • "ARCHITECT OF THE KING LEGACY" •
PEACE ACTIVIST & NONVIOLENT RESISTER

Growing up in segregated Alabama, Coretta Scott King's family home and timber mill were intentionally burned down by her white neighbors. A "disciplined nonconformist" all her life, she refused to let hate-filled acts hold her back. She picked cotton and waitressed to put herself through college, crediting her family and education for prepping her to take a stand when she found herself at the very center of the civil rights movement. The Montgomery Bus Boycott, sparked by Rosa Parks, established Coretta's pastor husband, Martin Luther King, Jr., as the movement's inspiring figurehead. Coretta stepped out as his committed partner in nonviolent social change. Just four days after Martin's assassination, she led a march of 50,000 people through Atlanta. The message? She was never going to back down from their courageous work. She founded a center and successfully lobbied for a national holiday that ensured her late husband's words and deeds remain among the most celebrated in American history.

Coretta's status as one of the world's most famous widows often obscures her own legacy as a human rights powerhouse. She was one of the earliest and loudest voices in the anti-nuclear and anti-Vietnam movements, a protester of South African Apartheid arrested alongside her children, and a faithful civil rights crusader for all walks of humanity.

"The hope of a secure and livable world lies with disciplined nonconformists . . . In any cause that concerns the progress of mankind, put your faith in the nonconformist!"

CORETTA SCOTT KING
CIVIL RIGHTS LEADER

Tenley Albright

BORN 1935

POLIO SURVIVOR • FIRST US WOMAN TO WIN FIGURE SKATING GOLD • SURGEON & CANCER RESEARCHER

As a child, Tenley Albright had two great ambitions: to become a doctor and to take home an Olympic gold medal. These aspirations were sparked when she won her first figure skating competition, just four months after her release from the hospital having been treated for polio. She worked toward both goals at once, hitting the rink by 4 a.m. to train before pre-med classes. By 1956, she had won two World titles but came up short of an Olympic victory. Two weeks before she competed in her second and final Winter Olympic Games, Tenley tripped on the ice and cut her ankle to the bone. Fighting back from the injury, she skated her way—stitches and all—to the top of the podium with memorable grace.

Tenley retired from skating to enroll in medical school, as one of only five women in her class. She brought the same absolute focus she learned on the ice rink to the operating room as a surgeon. Today, she's again combining arts and sciences as the founder of MIT Collaborative Initiatives, where diverse teams take on medical-social issues, from childhood obesity to post-traumatic stress disorder.

"If you don't fall down, you aren't trying hard enough."

TENLEY ALBRIGHT
FIGURE SKATER

Rose Marcario

BORN 1965

FINANCE WHIZ • MINDFUL LEADER • ENVIRONMENTAL INFLUENCER

After her parents' divorce left her mother on food stamps, Rose was driven to pursue a career that would ensure financial security. She steadily rose to the top of the world of high finance as the senior executive at a private equity firm, yet success did not bring her fulfillment. Taking a soul-searching break and studying Buddhism helped steer Rose towards a career more in tune with her values.

Inspired by the vision of Patagonia's eco-conscious founder, Rose signed on as an executive with the famous gear brand tailored for "silent sports" enthusiasts. She quickly established herself as a gutsy, respected leader. Her personal transformation has become the catalyst for a sustainable business revolution. Some of her innovations, achieved alongside her team, include making eco-friendly clothes designed to last a lifetime, building a recommerce platform for used goods, debuting a food line to encourage regenerative organic agriculture, and creating a hub to empower customers as activists. Profits have tripled, a confirmation that putting the planet first actually boosts the bottom line. As Patagonia racks up nods as one of the world's most innovative companies, Rose's all-in leadership is making sure it's one of the most conscious and influential, too.

"My whole self is here. My values, my passion, my sense of urgency."

ROSE MARCARIO

ACTIVIST CEO

Meghan Markle

BORN 1981

ACTOR • LIFESTYLE ENTREPRENEUR & PHILANTHROPIST • DUCHESS & MONARCHY MODERNIZER

Meghan Markle is living a real-life fairytale. This actor-turned-royal is more determined than ever to use her position as a platform. It's a commitment Meghan held from a very young age. At just eleven years old she led her first successful campaign for gender equality, lobbying Hillary Clinton and Gloria Steinem to help her get a sexist dish soap ad off the air. It took the young idealist a long time working odd jobs as a hostess and calligrapher to land her breakout role in the hit television drama, *Suits*. As soon as she did, Meghan put her celebrity toward global good works with clean water and girls' empowerment initiatives in Africa and India.

Recently married to British Royal, Prince Harry, Meghan's differences from the princess prototype—American, mixed-race, divorced—have made her a target for online bullying. But she's also earned countless fans as a true "People's Princess," akin to Harry's well-loved mom. Proving that she can rise above the noise, Meghan is embracing the title with her typical grace and genuineness. We can't wait to see the fruits of her fame.

"With fame comes opportunity, but it also includes responsibility— to advocate and share, to focus less on glass slippers and more on pushing through glass ceilings."

MEGHAN MARKLE
ROYAL

PURPOSE & CHANCE

Mildred "Babe" Didrikson Zaharias

1911–1956

THREE-TIME TRACK & FIELD MEDALIST • VAUDEVILLE STAR WHO TOURED AS THE "WORLD'S GREATEST WOMAN ATHLETE" • PRO GOLFER

Babe Didrikson grew up with one goal: to become the world's greatest athlete. As an all-rounder who played and excelled at practically everything except "dolls," she arguably made good on her grand ambition. Just 5'5" with an average frame, she wasn't an obvious contender to be the Greatest of All Time. Sure, Babe had natural ability, but her gutsiness, mental strength, and extraordinary drive to practice her way to the top secured her spot as an unrivaled sports legend.

Recruited out of high school to play basketball in an amateur league, Babe made headlines when she won the US women's track and field championships as a "one-girl team." Within three hours, she competed in eight events, placing first in six. At the 1932 Olympics, she broke four world records, taking medals in running, jumping, and throwing events—the only athlete ever to do so. She spent the rest of her career ruling the golf world. As a founding member of the Ladies Professional Golf Association, Babe used her visibility to help elevate the women's game to pro status. At the height of her career, she'd take five to six hours of lessons and drive more than a thousand balls a day before winding down with a few rounds of bowling. Her work ethic parlayed into eighty-two tournament wins, including fourteen in a row—a golf record, not likely to be broken anytime soon.

"Luck? Sure. But only after long practice and only with the ability to think under pressure."

BABE DIDRIKSON ZAHARIAS
ATHLETE

Eunice Kennedy Shriver

1921–2009

SOCIAL WORKER • CHILDREN'S HEALTH & DISABILITY RIGHTS
ADVOCATE • REVERED MEMBER OF A POLITICAL DYNASTY

Few people have impacted the lives of people with intellectual disabilities as much as Eunice Kennedy Shriver has. The social worker's sense of purpose came from bearing witness to the challenges of her beloved older sister, Rosemary, born with an intellectual disability. In Rosemary's honor, Eunice led the charge to create a network of research centers to study developmental disorders and medical ethics. She helped establish the National Institute for Child Health and Human Development. However, her greatest contribution was a knack for finding joyful ways to replace stigma and isolation with inclusive, confidence-building communities of support.

When Eunice heard from a disheartened mother that summer camps were refusing to admit her child, she opened a free month-long camp for children with developmental disabilities in her own backyard. Seeing campers delight in physical activity prompted Eunice to start the Special Olympics, a series of sporting events that got the public involved in her cause while offering friendship and support to athletes and their families. Founded in 1968, today the Special Olympics has grown to engage about four million athletes in one hundred and seventy-two countries. Providing year-round health care, training, and community programs, it's an organization with impact that carries well beyond the Games.

"Love produces confidence, and adversity produces purpose."

EUNICE KENNEDY SHRIVER
SPECIAL OLYMPICS FOUNDER

Sue Monk Kidd

BORN 1948

REGISTERED NURSE • SPIRITUAL MEMOIRIST • CONTEMPORARY VOICE OF SOUTHERN FICTION

With Sue Monk Kidd's late-breaking career as a best-selling novelist came living proof that it's never too late to realize your purpose. Her gift for weaving together words allows us, for a moment, to inhabit the lives of others, especially those with experiences very different from our own.

Sue had a real talent and zeal for creative writing as a child but let the pressure to do something practical bury her muse. Then, on her thirtieth birthday, she came down to breakfast and announced to her husband, who was juggling two hungry toddlers, that she was going to become a writer. Reclaiming her unique genius wasn't easy. She started as a freelancer, having some success with writing spirituality-driven articles and memoirs. Her first novel, *The Secret Life of Bees,* didn't come along until the age of fifty-three, but the book became an instant hit, selling millions of copies and inspiring adaptations for stage and screen. As a Georgia native who came of age during the civil rights movement, Sue often uses her lyrical voice to explore issues of gender and race. It's her way of fostering a global community in a world that could use more understanding.

"One of the more powerful outbreaks of happiness and meaning in your life will occur when you pair your passion and the world's need."

SUE MONK KIDD
NOVELIST

Sung-Joo Kim

BORN 1956

YOUNG REBEL • "CHIEF VISIONARY OFFICER" • GLOBAL BUSINESS
LEADER FIGHTING FOR WOMEN'S ECONOMIC EMPOWERMENT

Sung-Joo Kim got her entrepreneur DNA from her self-made CEO father, and her sense of purpose from her philanthropist mother. It's a combination that shaped her personal mantra and helped her redefine the core of twenty-first-century leadership as "caring and sharing."

Early on, Sung-Joo was disowned by her family for pursuing a career in the Western fashion industry when the expectation was for her to stay home and marry well. Her father was won over when an international deal landed them at the same negotiating table. The first-hand glimpse of Sung-Joo's win-win business acumen in action convinced him to invest in her dream of starting her own Korean conglomerate. Today, her multi-million-dollar enterprise, the Sunjoo Group, has revitalized the luxe handbag brand MCM and introduced iconic fashion labels to Asian markets. But it's her visible presence in humanitarian aid efforts and leadership in helping women worldwide to fashion their own success stories where her power shines brightest.

"Succeed to serve."

SUNG-JOO KIM

FASHION CEO

Debbie Millman

BORN 1962

AUTHOR-ARTIST & VISUAL STORYTELLER •
BRAND CONSULTANT & EDUCATOR • PODCASTING PIONEER

Debbie Millman discovered her love for design by chance. Hired as the arts and features editor for her university newspaper, the English major had an "aha" moment when she realized that designing the layout was her favorite part of the gig. She decided to run with her newfound passion, a fateful move that set her on course to becoming a renowned industry leader.

Always a Renaissance woman, Debbie has published visual essays, created editorial illustrations, and had her artwork displayed in exhibitions including at the famed Chicago Design Museum. The artist firmly believes branding is today's most influential creative medium, and she's taken that medium to new heights. She's penned some of the field's go-to how-to books and cofounded the world's first grad program in branding. She's the creator-host of one of the industry's first and longest running podcasts, *Design Matters*, and a leader of campaigns for many iconic global companies. Considered one of the world's most creative innovators, Debbie's proving that branding is much more than a logo or a look. It's a holistic art built from culture-sharing.

"If you imagine less, less will
be what you undoubtedly deserve.
Do what you love, and don't stop
until you get what you love."

DEBBIE MILLMAN
DESIGNER

Susan Wojcicki

BORN 1968

SILICON VALLEY NATIVE • ASPIRING ARTIST TURNED
TECH CREATOR • MODERN MARKETING WHIZ

Sometimes you chase down opportunities; sometimes they turn up unexpectedly on your doorstep. When Susan Wojcicki rented out her garage to a couple of computer science students, she had no idea that Google would be born there or that she would play a central role in the revolutionary tech titan. Susan was four months pregnant with her first child when she made the risky decision to quit her job at an established tech giant to join Google as their sixteenth employee. As the startup's first and only marketing person, with zero budget, she helped build a global, multi-billion-dollar brand that gave meaning to a made-up word.

Today, Susan is the head of YouTube, the world's largest video-sharing platform. She gives a voice to creators, nurtures niche communities, and encourages television disruptors to shake up the status quo. She's modeling how you grow a global business by focusing on what's next. Having had to be vocal to get her own name added to invite lists to be alongside deal-making giants, Susan's also working hard to ensure that women get an equal shot at shaping the future.

"Rarely are opportunities presented to you in the perfect way. In a nice little box with a yellow bow on top. 'Here, open it, it's perfect. You'll love it.' Opportunities—the good ones—are messy, confusing and hard to recognize."

SUSAN WOJCICKI
SOCIAL MEDIA CEO

HEART & MIND

Corita Kent

1918–1986

CATHOLIC SCHOOL GIRL • SOCIAL ACTIVIST • ART & EDUCATION INNOVATOR

Frances Elizabeth Kent, also known as Corita Kent or Sister Mary Corita, proved that time-honored faith and cutting-edge modern art can go hand-in-hand. When she became head of the art department at the Los Angeles convent-run college she herself had attended, Sister Mary Corita posted ten inspiring principles on her classroom wall. Among the avant-garde guidelines were playful reminders to encourage fearless experimentation, self-discipline, and whole-hearted engagement with one's work and world. Her rule of thumb about trust came in at number one.

Corita took vows straight out of high school, training as a Sister of the Immaculate Heart while earning degrees for art education. In grad school, Corita discovered screen printing, the ideal medium for ensuring her art was affordable and accessible. Her first glimpse of Andy Warhol's Campbell's Soup Cans made her a pop-art convert and shaped her signature style. Posing philosophical questions and bearing social justice messages, Corita's famously vibrant graphic and text prints were infused with a spirit of love and peace. Her memorable commissions included designing billboards, painting gas tanks, and creating the much-loved "Love" postage stamp. Though she eventually left the convent to pursue art full-time, Corita willed her entire estate to the Immaculate Heart Community. An art center and exhibitions carry her legacy forward.

"Find a place you trust and then try trusting it a while."

CORITA KENT
NUN & POP ARTIST

Jane Goodall

BORN 1934

CHIMPANZEE EXPERT • ENVIRONMENTALIST • UN MESSENGER OF PEACE

At just one year old, Jane Goodall was gifted with her favorite toy, Jubilee, a stuffed chimp named after a new addition to London Zoo. Twenty-five years later, British-born Jane parlayed her love of animals into a dream job of observing chimpanzees in Africa's Gombe Reserve. Armed with little more than binoculars and a notebook, Jane radically altered our understanding of primates.

Decades of patient and pioneering fieldwork revealed chimps' human-like behaviors, from their clever tool-making to complex emotional lives. Her research breakthroughs were captured on film by a *National Geographic* photographer named Hugo, who eventually became her first husband. Jane came away as the leading expert in her field, not to mention a Dame and one of the world's best-known scientists. Now in her eighties, Jane continues to head the research institute named after her while traveling some three hundred days per year to advocate for conservation and animal welfare. She founded a nonprofit organization called Roots & Shoots to engage a new generation of eco-warriors. Today, the youth empowerment movement has grown to eight thousand local chapters in one hundred and forty countries. She hopes to solve our most pressing scientific conundrums and save our planet by tapping into what's in our human hearts.

"Only when our clever brain and our human heart work together in harmony can we achieve our full potential."

JANE GOODALL
PRIMATOLOGIST

Anita Roddick

1942–2007

COSMETICS COMPANY FOUNDER • CONSCIOUS CAPITALIST • ADVOCATE FOR "BUSINESS AS UNUSUAL"

With an enterprise that grew from one modest Bristol, UK, storefront to more than two thousand locations, The Body Shop founder, Anita Roddick, was unquestionably a cosmetics industry giant. But the pioneering social entrepreneur's true business was empowerment. Mission-driven from day one, Anita dedicated her company to social and environmental change. She delivered on that vision by galvanizing customers, employees, and suppliers as her partners in a creative solution revolution. Dubbed "The Queen of Green," Anita's game-changing strategies pioneered ethical consumerism and paved the way for fair trade. For her, beauty products could be educational tools, and workplaces should be "incubators for the human spirit." Traveling provided opportunities to connect to new causes and broker community-sustaining deals with indigenous makers.

Anita hatched The Body Shop in 1976 to solve her own family's need. Left with two daughters while her equally adventuring husband trekked across the Americas, the startup business had to work. It was a matter of survival. Yet she never doubted that being on the front-lines of social responsibility and corporate citizenship was essential to making it a success. After thirty years at the helm, Anita sold The Body Shop to become a full-time activist. Determined not to "die rich," she poured her fortune into everything from anti-sweatshop campaigns to renewable energy.

"People become motivated when you guide them to the source of their power."

ANITA RODDICK
SOCIAL ENTREPRENEUR

Robin Roberts

BORN 1960

PIONEERING SPORTS BROADCASTER • BEST-SELLING AUTHOR •
AWARENESS RAISER

When breast cancer survivor Robin Roberts found out her cancer had resurfaced in the form of a rare blood disorder, it tested her instinctive optimism. The much-loved anchor rallied by living her mother's advice: "Make your mess your message." Bravely documenting her experience on camera and in print has given countless others strength to reach out for help, see their struggles through, and transform the way they think and feel.

Robin has had plenty of practice when it comes to perseverance. A tennis star and college basketball player, she's proof that the lessons learned from sports help you in life. When the pro career she longed for didn't happen, she became a trailblazing sportscaster instead. Her athletic savvy, work ethic and on-air ease helped her break into male-only broadcasting bastions like ESPN and NFL Primetime. Today, Robin's an Emmy-winning host of *Good Morning America*, a show she helped propel to the top of its time slot.

"Being optimistic is like a muscle that gets stronger with use . . . You have to change the way you think in order to change the way you feel."

ROBIN ROBERTS
TV ANCHOR

Elizabeth Cutler

BORN 1968

REAL ESTATE AGENT • CATALYST FOR STATIONARY BIKE RESURGENCE • EXPERIENCE-MAKER

When new moms Elizabeth Cutler and Julie Rice met for the very first time in 2006, they decided on the spot to launch a spin class startup in New York City. Coming out of that lunch meeting, former realtor Elizabeth tracked down their first Upper West Side studio on Craigslist while ex-talent scout Julie searched for sites to source the perfect plush towels. They didn't have backgrounds in entrepreneurship, formal fitness training, or venture capital funding. However, they did have vision, drive, crazy cofounder chemistry, and a conviction that creating a best-in-class exercise experience would turn customers into evangelists. With faithful followers and A-list clientele from Lady Gaga to Tom Cruise, Elizabeth and Julie's crazy venture has grown to eighty-five urban studios while creating a novel market for boutique fitness.

SoulCycle's secret to success was engineering an addictive exercise culture that was fresh, communal and fun, coached by charismatic instructors and fueled with energetic tunes. In 2016, Elizabeth and Julie sold their stake for a cool ninety million dollars. Elizabeth's latest project . . . another collaboration with Julie. Keep watching to see them bring what they've learned so far to discovering the next trend in living well.

"Culture is caught
and not taught."

ELIZABETH CUTLER
FITNESS ENTREPRENEUR

Maria Popova

BORN 1985

MARKETER • DIGITAL HUNTER-GATHERER • MODERN-DAY PHILOSOPHER

Originally from Bulgaria, Maria Popova was busy working four jobs to fund her college tuition in the United States when she embarked on a "tiny experiment." She began sending her advertising colleagues a weekly e-newsletter with a carefully selected handful of interesting items, from major scientific breakthroughs to little-known literary masterpieces, as heart and mind stimuli. Maria's "brain pickings" quickly went viral. They sparked a popular blog with a devoted fan-base and a spectrum of innovative web projects supported by avid readers. Eventually, her hobby developed into a career as a "curiosity architect" for her more than one million followers.

Along the way, Maria has helped define the aesthetics and ethics of digital curation. She's also become an envoy for "combinatorial creativity," the science-backed principle that engaging with a wide range of ideas from many different disciplines creates the cognitive scaffolding for powerful new thinking. Her takeaway from years spent collecting and sharing a kaleidoscope of perspectives? Practice generosity before you jump to critique. And, thinking creatively and critically means being open to changing your mind.

"It's infinitely more rewarding to understand than to be right—even if that means changing your mind about a topic, an ideology, or, above all, yourself."

MARIA POPOVA
BLOGGER

CONFIDENT & HUMBLE

Hattie McDaniel

1895–1952

WASHROOM ATTENDANT • RADIO STAR • TRAILBLAZING OSCAR WINNER

The youngest of thirteen children born to parents who had been slaves, this lifelong entertainer traveled with her brother's minstrel shows before landing in Hollywood. Almost always cast as a servant or slave, the hard-working Hattie appeared in more than three hundred films, yet never starred in any. Among her many talents, writing and singing the Blues. She's one of the rare performers with two stars on the Hollywood Walk of Fame—a nod to her popularity in radio and her big-screen success.

Though prejudice kept her from being cast as a leading lady or even from attending her own Atlanta premiere, she still left her mark on the entertainment industry. Her performance as Mammy in the year's epic best picture, *Gone with the Wind*, earned her the 1940 Academy Award for Best Supporting Actress. She secured her spot in film history as the first African American to win the coveted accolade. It took fifty-one years for the next African—American actress to take home an Oscar. The hunt goes on to locate the whereabouts of Hattie's long-lost—now very valuable—Academy Award (an engraved plaque, not today's widely known statuette).

"I've learned by livin' and watchin' that there is only eighteen inches between a pat on the back and a kick in the seat of the pants."

HATTIE MCDANIEL
ACTOR

Minerva Carcaño

BORN 1954

**THEOLOGIAN • COMMUNITY ORGANIZER •
IMMIGRANT RIGHTS ACTIVIST**

Minerva Carcaño would never have gotten to where she is today—as the first Latina bishop in the United States' second-largest Protestant denomination—if she had not been self-assured in her calling to pursue a life of faith and service. Her first experience of the holy spirit came early. Accompanying her father as he replaced the vinyl flooring in her church's kindergarten classroom, the five-year-old was suddenly overcome by the feeling of being "enveloped in God's love." This humble moment of grace guided her to become a Methodist pastor. Though the woman of God was initially met with resistance from family members and congregants, she made no attempt to "prove herself." Instead, Minerva simply lived her calling, knowing that understanding and mutual reverence would come.

Today, Minerva is an outspoken example of faith in action. A believer in a religious practice that addresses real-world needs, she isn't shy about taking up hot-button issues that affect her Southwest community. Herself a daughter of a Mexican farmworker, she feels called to give a voice to immigrants living in the "shadows of society." Minerva believes change is local. Gather people together to figure out issues in their own context, and they'll transform their own situations.

"Step out in the confidence that what is just and merciful will transform the situation."

MINERVA CARCAÑO
BISHOP

Judaline Cassidy

BORN 1972

PROUD TRADESWOMAN • PIONEERING UNION MEMBER • TEACHER OF FUTURE TRADESPEOPLE

As a four-foot-eleven woman in an industry that's dominated by men, Judaline Cassidy has had to bring real mettle to each building site, along with her tools. She has overcome unfounded bias by tackling tough jobs. Finally allowed into her local plumbers' union after a male member vouched for her, she became its first female leader. Now, she's eager to help other tradeswomen "own it" because they've earned it.

Being a plumber was not Judaline's childhood dream, but her native Trinidad & Tobago offered free training in the trades. What started as a means to pay the bills became her pursuit of a "noble craft" that's vital to the infrastructure of our everyday lives. Plus, as one of the few professions with pay equity, it's a darn good way to earn a living. Her union salary affords a lifestyle that allows her to provide for her family and impact her community. Among Judaline's charitable pursuits is an advisory role for NYC's Women's Building, a project that's transforming a former female prison into a creative space designed by women for women. She's also the founder of a nonprofit that's getting power tools (literally and figuratively) into girls' hands.

"I used to have this philosophy
of 'fake it till you make it.'
And now, I just own it."

JUDALINE CASSIDY

PLUMBER

Reese Witherspoon

BORN 1976

AMBASSADOR OF GRACIOUS SOUTHERN STYLE • OSCAR-WINNING MOVIE STAR • ACTOR-PRODUCER-ENTREPRENEUR ON A MISSION

When Reese Witherspoon was dubbed as one of *Glamour Magazine's* Women of the Year, she delivered a speech that went viral. Reese invited women and girls to embrace being go-getters and change-makers. Her point . . . ambition doesn't make you ruthless, selfish or unlikeable. It's a force for realizing your passions and for changing the world.

Reese is opening doors for other ambitious women. On screen, millions connected with her relatable humor and the message behind her iconic performance as the underestimated Elle Woods in *Legally Blonde*, a film that became an unexpected box office success. Since then, she's proved that investing in women-driven stories yields financial and social returns. She formed her own production and multi-media companies to fuel the demand for strong, complex female characters, bringing stories to light that might otherwise go unseen. She's ensuring women get meaty roles in front of and behind the camera. Reese is a leader among the leaders who are changing the societal circumstances that hold women back, not only in Hollywood, but across all industries.

"Ambition is not a dirty word. It's believing in yourself and your abilities. What would happen if we were all brave enough to be a little bit more ambitious? I think the world would change."

REESE WITHERSPOON
ACTOR

Dana Tanamachi

BORN 1985

MULTIDIMENSIONAL DESIGNER • TYPOGRAPHER • FAITHFUL RE-LEARNER

Graphic designer Dana Tanamachi's first job, creating modern-day Broadway show posters, inspired a love of vintage typography. Though trained in the latest design applications, when it came to fashioning her own fonts, she found hand-lettering much easier than mouse-clicking. Then, one night at a friend's party, a chalkboard wall gave her an artistic blank slate. Freed from her digital pen, she opened up a new imaginative landscape with dollar-store chalk. When friends saw her spontaneous typographic triumphs, they encouraged her to recognize and share her gift.

What came next? A chalk-art craze that generated high-profile commissions, including hotel branding, event installations, covers for *TIME* and *O Magazine,* and a classic children's book series—even a women's snowboard. As her reputation grew, Dana's fresh approach became increasingly mainstream until it was being copied and sold as a "Brooklyn aesthetic." Instead of banking on the well-established popularity of her style, Dana fell back on her mantra: "faithfulness over success." She reclaimed spontaneity by following her heart to small, slow and self-initiated projects, including an illuminated Bible and a gorgeous wall installation inviting everyone to "flourish." As Dana continues her artistic journey well beyond chalk, new clients have been more than willing to follow where her muse leads.

"Sometimes your limitations can be a launching pad into an unexpected story."

DANA TANAMACHI

ARTIST

Danielle Weisberg & Carly Zakin

DANIELLE BORN 1987 | CARLY BORN 1987

NEWS JUNKIES • ON-THE-JOB LEARNERS • SKIMM A & SKIMM B

The cofounders of *theSkimm*, Carly Zakin and Danielle Weisberg, have built an inventive content empire that's revolutionized how millennials stay informed. In the process, they've also set the standard for a confident-and-humble style of co-leadership. From the start, the two have run their fast-growing business with refreshing transparency. That means being up front about investments, letting everyone in on big "ahas" and publicly celebrating the wins. They're even honest about trials and missteps, blogging their top meltdowns and encouraging their team to fearlessly #failsohard because it's part of thinking big.

The now famous cofounders' close partnership has always been the core of their brand and key to their resilience. Quitting their day jobs as news producers, the former housemates pushed each other off the startup cliff. They went from poring over wire services to reimagining news delivery with theSkimm girl in mind. Carly and Danielle's innovation: creating a smart (and fun) way for young professionals to fit current events into their daily routines. They admittedly didn't know much about the business end of entrepreneurship, but they did know their audience. So well in fact, that their 6:15 a.m. email blast has about seven million subscribers. Now, they're scaling their signature voice and bringing it to social initiatives people, such as inspiring more than one hundred thousand people to register to vote.

"It's not healthy to keep a 'game face' on all the time . . . It's OK to have a meltdown. As leaders, the best example we can set is how to recover."

DANIELLE WEISBERG | CARLY ZAKIN
MILLENNIAL MEDIA INNOVATORS

COMMUNITY & SELF

Dolores Huerta

BORN 1930

ELEMENTARY SCHOOL TEACHER • SAVVY NEGOTIATOR •
HERO FOR WORKERS & "BORN-AGAIN FEMINIST"

Dolores Huerta has serious leadership cred. She's a cofounder and spokesperson for the United Farm Workers Union. Also an accomplished lobbyist and negotiator whose skills were so revered and feared, the opposition's team dubbed her the "Dragon Lady." A gifted speechmaker, she originated the empowering "¡Sí se puede!" ("Yes, we can!") slogan. One of her key messages is that we all have the potential to do what she has done. According to Dolores, inspiring leaders are made, not born.

She also believes that leadership isn't about top-down decision-making. Grassroots to her core, Dolores has always taken a bottom-up route to organizing. At age twenty-five, the former California school teacher became so discouraged by her students' poverty, she left her job to build a movement to better their families' lives. As a working-class mother with eleven children in the 1950s and 60s, she spent years fighting to secure higher wages, safer working conditions and a ban on child labor in agriculture. Her story has often been overshadowed by that of UFW cofounder Cesar Chavez or undermined by mudslingers. But today, the Presidential Medal of Freedom recipient is increasingly getting her due. Now in her late eighties, Dolores continues to spread the gospel of grassroots democracy while locking arms with a resurging feminist movement.

"People develop charisma in trying to reach people, in trying to get to them. Gradually and before you know it, you become a charismatic leader."

DOLORES HUERTA
LABOR LEADER

Cher

BORN 1946

UNINHIBITED POP LEGEND WITH UNIQUE CONTRALTO VOCALS •
ACADEMY AWARD WINNER • QUEEN OF THE COMEBACK

Cher dreamed of being famous before she knew how she was going to get there. She married songwriter Sonny Bono—eleven years her senior—when she was just a teen. As her producer, he kept a tight grip on her early career. They scored a number one hit with their 1965 folk-rock single "I've Got You Babe" and became household names with their massively popular show *The Sonny & Cher Comedy Hour*. When Cher decided it was time to go her own way, she suddenly realized that her husband essentially owned her brand, having a 95 percent stake in Cher Enterprises while their lawyer held the remaining 5 percent. Divorced and left with nothing, Cher did what she's now famous for: she reinvented herself.

Since then, Cher has unapologetically worn many hats (and wigs and even headdresses). Among them: fashion icon, pop goddess, acclaimed actress, infomercial celebrity, Vegas headliner, producer, and veterans' rights champion. Being a confident chameleon has often left her an "outsider" in the music and acting communities. But embracing her individuality has also yielded an Oscar, Emmy, Grammy, and three Golden Globes, not to mention made her the only recording artist with a number one track in each of the past six decades. Cher's gusty and glitzy self-stylings set the stage for today's stadium-filling divas (she's still one of them).

"All of us invent ourselves.
Some of us just have more
imagination than others."

CHER
POP STAR

Megan Smith

BORN 1964

THIRD EVER US CHIEF TECHNOLOGY OFFICER • SERIAL COLLABORATOR •
WOMEN IN TECH HISTORY BUFF

Self-described tech evangelist Megan Smith is a pro at heading teams that use technology to solve the world's most complex problems. Her formula for driving innovation is simple: finding people to wonder with.

Megan first experienced the power of creative collaboration as a young engineer. She pitched in on projects that included everything from solar cookstoves to an award-winning bike lock, space stations to smartphones. Since then, Megan's continued to scale her teamwork for social good with an astonishing list of cocreations like The Malala Fund, Google's "SolveForX" and "Women Techmakers" initiatives, and the United Nation's Solutions Summit. When tapped by the White House to become the US's "top techie," she focused on empowering more collaborators by "debugging" unconscious bias and pushing for policies designed to make coding as commonplace as learning the ABCs. Today, Megan's finding fresh ways to unlock our collective genius as cofounder of shift7, an organization whose motto is "solution making through inclusion." Her personal passion . . . uncovering the forgotten stories of women in the science, technology, engineering, and math industries, from programming pioneer Ada Lovelace to NASA mathematician Katherine Johnson.

"Find astonishing people and hang out with them."

MEGAN SMITH
TECH EXECUTIVE

Kelly Holmes

BORN 1970

MILITARY VET & ARMY JUDO CHAMP • TWO-TIME OLYMPIC GOLD MEDALIST • DAME & MENTAL HEALTH ADVOCATE

Kelly Holmes showed her toughness from day one. Born to a young, single mother, she grew up in a working-class family. A teacher helped summon her unique athletic talents, fueling her passion for sports. She joined Great Britain's Royal Army Corps to pursue a career as a physical trainer but ended up being assigned to drive a four-ton truck instead. When competing—and winning—in military races dominated by men, she decided to take her running career international. Ten years later, at the age of thirty-four, she battled back from a series of potentially career-ending injuries to take home two gold medals for Great Britain in the Athens Olympics. Only after achieving her dream did Kelly give voice to how hard a journey it had been. Her championship spirit masked the many down days and made her reluctant to reach out when she most needed help. In fact, her depression and self-harm reached their height just one year before her legendary victories.

Today, Kelly's toughness shows up by revealing her vulnerabilities instead of masking them. Her story breaks the silence surrounding mental health issues. Through her foundation, she's encouraging everyone, from young offenders to full-time caretakers, to deliberately build a community of support.

"Create 'Team You'."

KELLY HOLMES
OLYMPIC RUNNER

Jessica Jackley

BORN 1977

SOCIAL ENTREPRENEUR • CATALYST FOR DEVELOPING COMMUNITIES •
GLOBAL DO-GOODER

Jessica Jackley always wanted to help take on poverty, but traditional philanthropy left her feeling overwhelmed, guilty, and distant from people in need. She found a solution when she discovered microfinance, financial and banking services that offer a hand up to low-income individuals and communities. Following one of her own favorite bits of advice, "run toward the things you love," Jessica quit her job and took a research trip to East Africa to see how she could help. Soon after, she cofounded the first worldwide, peer-to-peer microlending marketplace. With more than one billion dollars raised and nearly three million life-saving loans issued, Kiva is still going strong.

Jessica remains a sought-after advocate for economies based on sharing and participating in each others' stories. This philosophy and poetry major has discovered that her fundamental beliefs go hand-in-hand with many of the big thinkers she studied. By understanding the dreams and daily happenings of humble business owners—goat herders, fishermen, dressmakers—we can create empowering partnerships that enable them to grow on their own terms. She remains on the lookout for the next big project that will empower entrepreneurs as they seek a better life.

"Being dedicated to someone else or to a group of people will make you your best self."

JESSICA JACKLEY
MICROFINANCE PIONEER

Natalie Franke

BORN 1990

WEDDING PHOTOGRAPHER TURNED CREATIVE COMMUNITY CATALYST • "LEFT-BRAIN GIRL IN A RIGHT-BRAIN WORLD" • BRAIN TUMOR WARRIOR

Natalie Franke was raised in a right-brain family of scientists. When she fell in love with photography, she decided to study the science behind left-brain creativity while growing her own business. It didn't take long for her to grasp the day-in-day-out struggles that come with being a creative solopreneur. Instead of accepting cutthroat competition and individual success as the rules of the game, she set out to redefine the creative industry. In 2015, she launched The Rising Tide Society, an organization that quickly made waves, growing to one hundred thousand members in just eighteen months. Meetups—known as #TuesdaysTogether—sprung up around the world. Natalie's call for #CommunityOverCompetition became the connective tissue among creatives, entrepreneurs, and innovators, all yearning for timely education, no-nonsense technologies, and a genuinely collaborative support network.

When Natalie recently underwent brain surgery to remove a benign tumor, the community she helped foster stepped up to back her recovery while keeping her good work going. Today, she's returned with renewed purpose to the hustle she loves: "building a business to build a life" and helping others do the same.

"All tides rise when we support one another in pursuit of our dreams."

NATALIE FRANKE
COMMUNITY BUILDER

WANDER & WONDER

Isabella Bird

1831–1904

POPULAR TRAVEL WRITER & PHOTOGRAPHER •
HOSPITAL COFOUNDER • THE ORIGINAL SOLO-TRAVELER

England-born writer Isabella Bird suffered from chronic ill health. When her doctor suggested recuperating in warmer climates, she turned the prescription into a new lease on life. She went from being a frail middle-aged woman prone to headaches and insomnia to one of the Victorian era's most intrepid and famous world travelers. Not fussed about creature comforts or lady-like appearances, Isabella put in thousands of miles on foot, horseback, and ocean steamers, venturing along "unbeaten tracks" and even into warzones. She embraced the rugged outdoors, be it trekking through the Rocky Mountains with a one-eyed desperado for her guide or riding an elephant through the Malay jungle.

From the Americas to the Far East, Isabella's globe-trotting adventures made for best-selling books. At sixty, she took up photography, earning praise for her excellent technique in the trickiest conditions. She soon put it into practice during a dangerous expedition to document everyday life in China. Her astute and admiring chronicle is credited with introducing the unfamiliar country to Western audiences. Today, she's remembered as the first female fellow admitted into the Royal Geographical Society, as cofounder of two hospitals in India and as an icon of independence who was a literal trailblazer.

"I have found far more than I ever dared to hope for."

ISABELLA BIRD
EXPLORER

Vera Rubin

1928–2016

YOUNG STARGAZER • ASTROPHYSICS RESEARCHER & NATIONAL MEDAL OF SCIENCE HOLDER • GRAND DAME OF DARK MATTER

Celebrated astronomer Vera Rubin shed light on what we can't see, even through high-powered telescopes. In the 1970s, Vera confirmed the existence of "dark matter," a mysterious invisible substance that, according to her calculations, accounted for a whopping 90 percent of a galaxy's mass. Her monumental discoveries forever changed our view of the cosmos.

Vera was a trailblazer whose immigrant parents encouraged her to pursue science at a time when teachers and fellow colleagues were actively discouraging her from doing so. Nevertheless, Vera built her own telescope as a teen and graduated from Vassar, the same university where her muse, the comet-discovering Maria Mitchell, once taught. She was the only astronomy major in her class. Many thought her body of work merited a Nobel prize, but Vera cared less about personal fame than her numbers. She was also passionate about mentoring generations of women to push the frontiers of knowledge. With only a tiny percentage of the universe being made up of matter we can see and understand, there remains plenty of mysterious in-between to explore.

"Don't shoot for the stars, we already know what's there. Shoot for the space in between because that's where the real mystery lies."

VERA RUBIN
ASTRONOMER

Chita Rivera

BORN 1933

TRIPLE-THREAT (DANCER-SINGER-ACTOR) • TWO-TIME TONY WINNER •
BROADWAY LEGEND

This iconic stage performer may be well past the typical retirement age, but she's still not ready to settle down or rest on her laurels. Chita Rivera crooned, leapt and high-kicked her way into American pop culture, as a stereotype-breaking and era-defining leading lady.

Chita's parents tried to channel her boundless energy by enrolling her in ballet classes. Scouted to audition for the American School of Ballet, she studied under choreographer George Balanchine from the age of sixteen. At nineteen, she translated her classical training to musicals, pairing her technical backbone with a new freedom of expression. After putting in the time on tours and revues, Chita created the role of Anita in the 1957 Broadway debut of *West Side Story*. Since then, her name has been regularly in lights. Not even the car accident that left her leg shattered—surgically pieced back together using sixteen metal screws—could keep her off tour for long. (At the time, it took seven chorus girls to replace her.) A two-time Tony winner, her last nomination came in 2015 at age eighty-two, ten years after she made history as the first Latina to receive a Kennedy Center Honor.

"What do you want to stop for? You don't want to get roots; they pull you down."

CHITA RIVERA
MUSICAL THEATER STAR

Naomi Shihab Nye

BORN 1952

SONGWRITER • AWARD-WINNING CHILDREN'S AUTHOR • "WANDERING POET"

Naomi Shihab Nye has long carried around a scrap of paper with poet laureate Philip Levine's take on the creative muse. He describes it as "the portion of the self that largely lives asleep" whereas "being inspired is really being totally alive." For more than 40 years, Naomi has traveled the world to help people awaken to that odd and delicious state. Meanwhile, her global sojourns, daily mullings and chance encounters have found expression through her own poetry and more than thirty published books.

The daughter of a Palestinian refugee, Naomi was born four years after her father's family lost their home in Jerusalem. The feeling of exile became part of day-to-day life in their new Missouri home. It helped Naomi find her voice as a wandering poet from a very early age. As a teen, Naomi lived in the West Bank for a year, kindling her artistic interest in using cultural exchange to address tense social conflicts. Today, the creative writing teacher has extended her repertoire to bridge-building storybooks and young adult novels centered on the ordinary lives of Arab Americans. It's work that carries on the spirit of her poetry, inviting people to reconsider what we normally overlook, in the world and inside ourselves.

"I love staring, pondering, mulling, puttering. I love the times when someone or something is late–there's that rich possibility of noticing more, in the meantime."

NAOMI SHIHAB NYE
POET

Lisa Lutoff-Perlo

BORN 1956

SEAPORT NATIVE • LOYAL LADDER-CLIMBER •
FIRST FEMALE CEO OF PUBLICLY TRADED CRUISE LINE

When Lisa Lutoff-Perlo joined the sales team of a cruise line, her dream was to one day head the department. Seventeen years later, she was transitioned to a marketing role, then, to oversee all business operations. Initially, Lisa felt like her career was steering off course, but the mentors promoting her out of her comfort zone had a well-founded belief in her leadership. Having learned the hospitality business from the bottom to the top over three decades, she was appointed president and CEO of Celebrity Cruises in 2014. Her first move as a top executive was to pay it forward. Lisa asked a gifted female mariner to join her by becoming a ship captain, signaling her commitment to go beyond mentorship and actively sponsor promising up-and-comers.

Besides being at the table while designing ultra-cool next-generation cruise ships and experiences that redefine modern luxury, Lisa's using her time at the helm to usher in a cultural seachange. Always conscientious about creating a welcoming environment for travelers, now Lisa's working to diversify the bridge (which was made up of just 5 percent of women when she initially took over). With employees from fifty countries working together to take people to destinations in all seven continents, this high-impact leader is encouraging the world to "sail beyond borders."

> "Would you like to join me on this journey?"

LISA LUTOFF-PERLO
CRUISE LINE CEO

Kate McCue

BORN 1978

AVID DIVER & LIFELONG SEA ADVENTURER • MASTER MARINER • US'S FIRST FEMALE CRUISE SHIP CAPTAIN

Kate McCue's parents took her on a cruise to the Bahamas as a kid. She came away from their adventure with a new career ambition: to become a cruise director. Her father reminded her that she could be anything she wanted, including the ship's captain, and she began imagining taking the wheel instead. Kate's unconventional undergrad experience at the California Maritime Academy equipped her with business knowhow plus a marine license to captain anything from a tugboat to a supertanker. Setting her sights on the cruise industry, she signed on as a third officer and quickly rose through the ranks. At thirty-seven, Kate's dream came true when fellow trailblazer, newly minted cruise line CEO Lisa Lutoff-Perlo, named Kate captain of her first mega-ship.

As master of a cruise ship, Kate's gig goes well beyond mid-sea maneuvers and docking at tricky ports of call (though she's an ace at both). Kate and her crew have piloted new culinary and entertainment experiences, safely escorted passengers from the Caribbean to Canada, and even received a humanitarian award for their lifesaving rescue of sailors stranded at sea.

"My motto about the unknown is: You never know if you want it until you try it. So, when you see an opportunity, seize it. When you spot a problem, fix it. When you want something, ask for it."

KATE MCCUE
SHIP CAPTAIN

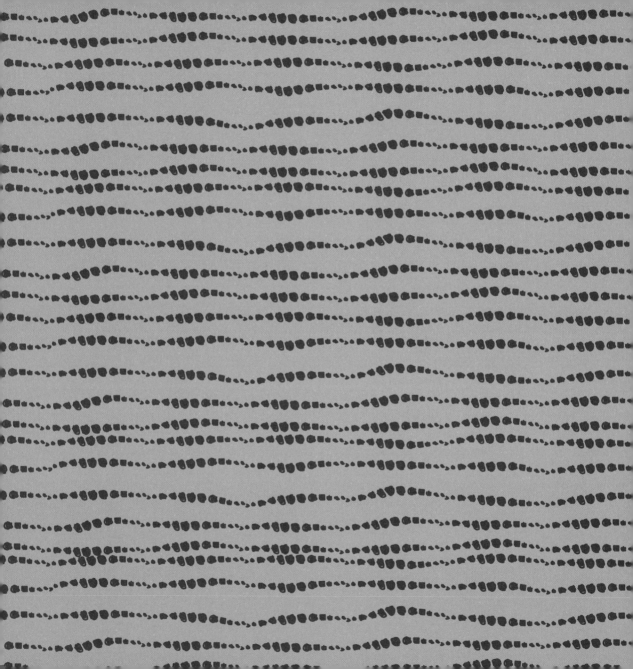

IMAGINE **&** DO

Beatrix Potter

1866–1943

NATURALIST • FARM MANAGER • BELOVED CHILDREN'S AUTHOR

London-born Beatrix Potter grew up sketching the flora and fauna of the English countryside where her family went on holiday. Her childhood fascination with nature was the north star of her pursuits. She moonlighted as a mushroom expert and ran fifteen farms, was the first woman elected president of the Herdwick Sheep Breeders' Association, and donated four thousand lush acres to be preserved and enjoyed. She's best known for her imaginative renderings of mischievous and smartly dressed animals. She bound them in children's storybooks, sized perfectly for small hands.

Beatrix had already developed into an accomplished commercial illustrator when she mailed a fateful letter featuring a charming picture story to five-year-old Noel, her former governess's son. The tale, inspired by one of her pets—a Belgian buck rabbit named Peter Piper—turned into the first in a series of childhood classics. After multiple rejections, she self-published *Peter Rabbit*. Its instant popularity made publishers reconsider. Today, it has sold forty million copies. Always business savvy, Beatrix took Peter to the patent office, making him the oldest licensed literary character. At the forefront of merchandising, she introduced stylish games, plush toys, and tea sets starring her furry and feathered friends. More than a century on, Beatrix's lovable menagerie graces nurseries worldwide.

"What heaven can be more real than to retain the spirit-world of childhood, tempered and balanced by knowledge and common sense."

BEATRIX POTTER
AUTHOR-ILLUSTRATOR

Condoleezza Rice

BORN IN 1954

CONCERT PIANIST • SOVIET UNION EXPERT • POLITICAL SCIENCE PROFESSOR

Condoleezza Rice grew up in one of the most segregated cities in the United States. But her teacher-parents taught her about the transformative power of education in breaking down barriers. Though Condoleezza's early ambition was to be a professional pianist, in college, she discovered a passion for political science while taking a course taught by Madeleine Albright's father. Being open to this unexpected turn in the road set her on a path to becoming a leading Soviet expert, celebrated scholar, and the first African-American woman to serve as US Secretary of State. During her tenures as a national security advisor and the country's top diplomat, Condoleezza was a key player in the US response to major international conflicts such as the fall of the Soviet Union, the reunification of Germany, the 9/11 attacks, and the Iraq War.

Now, following in her parents' footsteps, the educator is using her global experience to advise up-and-coming leaders. And she's clocking more firsts in a very different arena—sports. One of the first women granted membership at Augusta National Golf Club, Condoleezza was also the first female appointee to the College Football Playoff Selection Committee. Many would like to see this lifelong Browns fan score another first (plus, her dream job) as the next NFL commissioner.

"People who end up as 'first' don't actually set out to be first. They set out to do something they love."

CONDOLEEZZA RICE
SECRETARY OF STATE

Beth Cross

BORN 1959

HORSE LOVER & AVID RIDER • BUSINESS STRATEGIST • FAR-SIGHTED FOUNDER

When business strategist Beth Cross decided to start her own company, she and cofounder Pam Parker were clear on the endgame: to become the world's premier equestrian footware and apparel brand. Inspired by an early investor, they took time to map out what that company would look like. Their belief in Ariat's potential helped identify ideal customers, employees, and investors to actualize their vision.

The idea for Ariat was hatched while Beth was working on accounts for two athletic footwear giants. She had grown up on a horse farm in Pennsylvania with her own string of ponies. She loved riding both English and Western. Though modern riders were elite athletes, the available performance gear was long out of date. She decided it was time to apply the technologies being used for other sports to innovate equestrian footwear—and then apparel—without compromising comfort or style. After launching the world's most technically advanced riding boot, Beth brought in other passionate rider-designers to expand their cutting-edge offerings. Today, Ariat has made good on its founders' early resolve. They've gotten there through a deep knowledge of and investment in their niche.

"You cannot delegate vision."

BETH CROSS
EQUESTRIAN GEAR INNOVATOR

Jeni Britton Bauer

BORN 1970

AMATEUR PERFUMER • B CORP FOUNDER • FLAVOR IMAGINEER

Cocoa-curry-coco. Ricotta toast with red berry geranium jam. Genmaicha and marshmallows. These are just a few of the intriguingly unique blends that have made flavor mastermind Jeni Britton Bauer an ice cream mogul. The art student founded her namesake business in 2002 on a seemingly simple mission: make better ice cream. Nearly two decades, thirty scoop shops, and a James Beard Award-winning cookbook later, Jeni's still on a quest to perfect the art and chemistry of her sweet trade. She works directly with a carefully cultivated fellowship of growers and makers to craft every batch with milk from grass-grazed cows. Famous for her seasonal collections, she mixes in Ohio wildflower honey, whole fruits and veggies, herbs from nearby farms, as well as rare, carefully sourced ingredients from around the world.

Thirteen years in, Jeni's smile-inspiring operations almost came to a halt. A food bacteria scare shut down her kitchen (no one got sick). She got through the crisis by acting with speed, transparency, and extreme caution, putting customers first while leaning on her community. At the end of the day, her taste-bud-enchanting work is about bringing people together.

"Forward is not a straight line. It's much more exciting, complex, difficult, gnarly, and uncharted than that."

JENI BRITTON BAUER
ARTISAN ICE CREAM MAKER

Milka Duno

BORN 1972

MODEL • NAVAL ENGINEER • STOCK CAR DRIVER

Milka Duno has never stayed in her lane when it comes to society's expectations. A Venezuelan model and qualified Naval engineer, she earned four masters degrees in maritime business and aquaculture, working on three simultaneously. Then an invite to a driving clinic hosted by a sports car club sparked a new passion. At age twenty-four, it was late to be coming to the sport, but Milka didn't let inexperience keep her from taking to the racetrack and striving for pro status in one of the few sports where men and women go head-to-head. Instead, she let her focus and determination motor her to become one of the world's most successful and versatile female drivers.

In her US debut in 2000, Milka topped the podium at the Miami Grand Prix as the first woman to peg a major race win in the United States. A decade later at age forty-two, she crossed the finish line on another goal, becoming NASCAR's first Latina driver. Milka added film actress to her creds, playing Kellie Gearbox in the live-action adaptation of *Speed Racer.* Once known for cruising at speeds faster than two hundred miles per hour, these days Milka keeps her foot on the gas pedal by helping young people chase academic excellence.

"Forget the competition and focus on your goal."

MILKA DUNO
RACE CAR DRIVER

Mikaila Ulmer

BORN 2005

BIG DREAMER • BEE AMBASSADOR • KID KEYNOTER & CHANGE AGENT

The ultimate rookie, Mikaila Ulmer was just four years old when she signed up for a young entrepreneurs' fair. The only problem? She needed a product. The innovative solution came from a surprising place: a recipe for her Great-Granny Helen's flaxseed lemonade published in a 1940s cookbook. The delicious drink was sweetened with honey, a simple ingredient that supplied a key learning moment. Twice stung by bees in just one week, Mikaila didn't have a very high opinion of the industrious pollinators and honey-makers. When she found out more about their eco-importance, it inspired the young social entrepreneur to dream up a way to protect their dwindling populations.

Mikaila founded Me & the Bees Lemonade, using her great-granny's recipe. Presenting her business plan on the show *Shark Tank* when she was just ten years old, she won a sixty-thousand-dollar investment to get her startup off the ground. Soon after, she landed a multi-million-dollar deal with Whole Foods to carry her better-for-you, better-for-the-planet line. Each sale raises awareness and funds for bee charities. The teen is already becoming a serial entrepreneur with more products for good. Her message to leaders of every age? Tap into your inner child. Then, you'll be able to see endless possibilities.

"Dream like a kid."

MIKAILA ULMER
TEEN ENTREPRENEUR

TRADITION INNOVATION

FANNIE FARMER

1857–1915

TEEN STROKE SURVIVOR • COOKING SCHOOL PRINCIPAL •
"MOTHER OF LEVEL MEASUREMENTS"

In 1896, Fannie Farmer forever changed American kitchens. How? By giving us "definite guides." Besides offering an encyclopedic collection of twelve hundred classic dishes (think: forty-three ways to make potatoes), Fannie's landmark *Boston Cooking-School Cook Book* modernized recipe standards. Instead of a haphazard handful of this or a dash of that, she introduced level measurements, detailed instructions, and nutritional information alongside lists of ingredients. Fannie's novel teaching move meant cookery was no longer domestic drudgery or high art. Instead, it was a serious science—one that anyone could master, given the right tools and training.

Forced to leave school as a teen to recover from a stroke, Fannie took up cooking to convert her family's home into a boarding house. At thirty-one, she enrolled in the Boston Cooking School. A better "promoter and businesswoman" than even a cook, Fannie became the school's principal, transforming the onetime charity into a fashionable, profitable culinary mecca. Nevertheless, publishers made her pay to print her first cookbook for fear it would flop. Selling over three hundred thousand copies during her lifetime, the book made Fannie famous—a sought-after lecturer with a school bearing her name. New Fannie Farmer cookbooks are still released today, adding fresh recipes to old favorites like steamed brown bread and Boston baked beans.

"GOOD JUDGMENT, WITH EXPERIENCE, HAS TAUGHT SOME TO MEASURE BY SIGHT; BUT THE MAJORITY NEED DEFINITE GUIDES."

FANNIE FARMER
CULINARY PIONEER

TU YOUYOU

BORN 1930

PHARMACEUTICAL CHEMIST • TRADITIONAL MEDICINE SCHOLAR •
"THE MODEST NOBEL LAUREATE"

At age eighty-four, Tu Youyou became the first Chinese scientist to win the Nobel Prize in Medicine for leading a team that discovered a new therapy to halt the global malaria epidemic. Youyou's innovation? A return to a two-thousand-year-old Chinese tradition of herbal medicine. Her thoughtful combination of age-old wisdom with state-of-the-art techniques sparked one of the greatest modern medical achievements, affecting hundreds of millions of people worldwide.

Surviving tuberculosis as a teen got Youyou interested in medical research. In 1967, the young scientist was entrusted with a top-secret mission to find a lifesaving remedy. It was the Vietnam War era, and malaria was killing more soldiers than combat. Meanwhile, China's Cultural Revolution was leaving scientists sidelined and resources scarce. Scouring ancient Chinese medical texts, Youyou turned up artemisinin, a sweet wormwood extract that inhibits the malaria parasite. A simultaneous US military project tested about two hundred thousand compounds with no success. She got the drug out of her labs by volunteering to become its first human test subject. Youyou's heroic contribution might have remained overlooked had it not been for the curiosity of two contemporary malaria researchers. After a few years of digging, they published artemisinin's unlikely origin story, raising Youyou from an underrated professor (long denied entrance into the Chinese Academy of Sciences) to one of China's most celebrated scientists.

"WE HAVE A PRECIOUS WEALTH FROM OUR ANCIENT TIMES."

TU YOUYOU
CHEMIST

VERA WANG

BORN 1949

FIGURE SKATER TURNED FASHION EDITOR • WEDDING GOWN REVOLUTIONARY • LIFESTYLE MOGUL

New Yorker Vera Wang was determined to have a career as a competitive figure skater. When her 1968 Olympic dreams were cut short, she channeled the grace and discipline she'd learned on the rink into a new field—fashion. At twenty-three, Vera became the youngest ever senior editor at *Vogue*. After two decades supporting design icons, the industry insider made a gutsy career move that rewrote the rules on bridal wear.

Inspired by her own frustrating search for something other than a flouncy, princess frock that didn't suit the forty-year-old bride, Vera set out to fill a serious gap. Her market: soon-to-be-brides yearning for chic, modern gowns. Little did she know, doing "bridal" came with a stigma attached. It initially cost Vera her "insider" status in the fashion world, but twenty-five years of blissfully happy brides later, she's one of its best-known names. Along the way, she has drawn on classic design elements while constantly redefining the traditional wedding dress with daringly deconstructed, asymmetrical, and colorful styles. Today, Vera's pioneering label is synonymous with luxe couture weddings and gorgeous modern gowns. She's also venturing far beyond a woman's big day to translate her vision "out." With lines of ready-to-wear apparel, jewelry, housewares, and stationery, Vera is making high fashion accessible.

"I NEED TO KNOW WHAT COMES BEFORE SO I CAN BREAK THE RULES."

VERA WANG
FASHION DESIGNER

MARY BARRA

BORN 1961

ELECTRICAL ENGINEER • FIRST FEMALE CEO OF A MAJOR
AUTOMAKER • CHAMPION FOR GIRLS IN STEM AND MANUFACTURING

Mary Barra's father was a die maker at a General Motors car factory
for thirty-five years, instilling in his daughter an appreciation for old-
fashioned hard work. She first joined the company as a "factory rat" to
help fund her engineering degree. Today, Mary has not only surpassed
her dad's tenure at the auto industry giant, but she's also become its top
executive. She never expected to find herself in the driver's seat, but
staying laser-focused on excelling at the job at hand kept her cruising—
from inspecting fenders on the factory floor to overseeing the company's
global supply chains and product offerings. When she was tapped to
take the wheel, the company was still reeling from bankruptcy and facing
a recall scandal that compromised public trust. The loyal and practical
Mary seemed like a safe pair of hands. And she has been, taking the
company back to solid returns by restoring a culture of quality, integrity,
accountability, and innovation.

Protecting timeless values has actually enabled Mary to drive her
supercentenarian organization to become the car company of the future,
setting the vision for a "zero crashes, zero emissions, zero congestion"
world. With investments in ride-sharing, self-driving, and all-electric tech,
Mary is reshaping the image of GM to a frontrunner that's reimagining
how we come and go.

"NOT EVERYTHING NEEDS CHANGING. SOME THINGS NEED PROTECTING. AND THAT CAN BE JUST AS IMPORTANT, CHALLENGING AND REWARDING AS CHANGING THE WORLD."

MARY BARRA
AUTO INDUSTRY CEO

WENDY KOPP

BORN 1967

UNDERGRAD WITH A VISION • NONPROFIT EXECUTIVE •
ORGANIZER OF HOPE-FILLED ROOKIE TEACHERS

Distressed by inequalities in education, Wendy Kopp used her 1989 college thesis to propose a solution—a national teaching corps. She envisioned a movement of emerging leaders channeling their talents toward teaching in low-income urban and rural public schools. When the new grad struck out on the job market, she decided to act on her crazy idea. A professor famously dismissed her ambition as "deranged." Investors were likewise skeptical. But Wendy knew there were legions of new grads looking for meaningful work and longing to make a difference. She proved the concept and won backers when her grassroots campus recruitment effort generated twenty-five hundred applicants in just four months. Since then, Teach for America has enlisted more than fifty-five thousand newly minted graduates to create opportunities for many of the United States' most disadvantaged students. The program's earned its reputation as an incubator for future leaders. Tens of thousands of TFA alums who now work across all industries remain passionate, active participants in closing the education gap.

In 2007, Wendy decided to do it all again, founding the international network Teach for All to collaborate globally on tackling local inequalities. The proven leader was surprised to meet with the same naysaying she had as a rookie. The lesson? "The rare souls who choose to say 'yes' have an outsized impact."

"THERE'S A HUGE POWER
IN INEXPERIENCE.
YOU JUST DON'T KNOW
WHAT'S IMPOSSIBLE, AND
THEREFORE THINK,
'OF COURSE THIS CAN
BE DONE!'"

WENDY KOPP
EDUCATION CORPS FOUNDER

AYANNA HOWARD

BORN 1972

ELECTRICAL ENGINEER • PERSONAL ROBOT IMAGINEER •
ED TECH FOUNDER

Less than 20 percent of engineers are women; only 5 percent are African American. Computer engineering professor Ayanna Howard has designs to boost those numbers. Her startup "gamifies" STEM education by creating inclusive toys for kids as young as three. She's ensuring kids become comfortable with code while growing up seeing opportunities to become science pros. Her team's initiatives go beyond fun and games. According to Ayanna, changing the face of STEM ensures a pipeline of the diverse skills and perspectives necessary to creatively address heady challenges.

The rising star of robotics' personal inspiration? *The Bionic Woman*, a 1970s-era TV show in which the title character comes back from a critical injury with superhero-like powers after being fitted with cybernetic limbs. Now, Ayanna is busy making what was once sci-fi into reality. Always fascinated by the relationship between humans and robots, she has spent her career equipping our programmable friends with smarts to think, act, and make ethically informed decisions. Among her projects—a self-directed Mars rover, computer vision to help machines decode digital images, and a pair of robotic hands that know how to change shape and grasp objects. Today, Ayanna heads her own human-automation lab, leading the way to a not-so-distant future where personal robots will be as common as cell phones.

"BE CONFIDENT THAT YOUR DIFFERENCE IS WHAT MAKES YOUR ABILITY TO INNOVATE UNIQUE."

AYANNA HOWARD
ROBOTICIST

TRAINING & INSTINCT

Maria Montessori

1870–1952

PHYSICIAN • ACCLAIMED EDUCATION RESEARCHER & SCHOOL FOUNDER • NURTURER OF OUR INBORN CURIOSITY

Besides being the first woman ever to graduate from medical school in Italy, Maria Montessori was a big thinker in the field of early childhood education. Her scientifically grounded approach transformed traditional classrooms by catering to children's natural curiosity. The face of twentieth-century education reform, Maria opted out of heavy-handed lectures, strict discipline, religious doctrine, and teacher-led lessons. Instead, she gave students the space and freedom to learn in self-directed, experience-based ways. The result? Independent kids who developed their senses and individuality along with their intellects.

After years of testing, Maria debuted her child-centered style of teaching in 1907 in an underserved area of Rome. Her methods had an immediate international impact, spawning congresses, associations, Montessori schools on five continents, and publications translated into twenty languages. Often traveling to help spread her insights, Maria began a three-month-long trip to India that ended up lasting seven years when World War II left her stranded. While there, she personally trained a thousand teachers and found a new, solemn reason for her calling: education as "the best weapon for peace." More than a century after the Montessori Method first went viral, there are still more than twenty thousand schools worldwide that bear her name and countless others that apply her time-tested practices of tapping into each child's inner drive to learn.

"The best instruction
is that which uses
the least words
sufficient for the task."

MARIA MONTESSORI
EDUCATOR

Maria Tallchief

1925–2013

ARTISTIC DIRECTOR • CHICAGO BALLET FOUNDER • THE ORIGINAL SUGAR PLUM FAIRY

Named "Woman of Two Worlds" by her Oklahoma Osage tribe, Maria Tallchief helped spread an Old-World art in the New World as the United States' first major prima ballerina. Leaping into a scene dominated by Russian dancers, the dedicated student won a spot with the prestigious touring troupe the Ballet Russe when she was just seventeen. There, her dynamic solos caught the eye of legendary choreographer George Balanchine, who invited Maria to help launch the New York City Ballet in 1948. She became the company's inaugural principal dancer (plus George's muse and onetime wife).

Maria won hearts on a grand scale when she created the role of the Sugar Plum Fairy in a 1954 revival of *The Nutcracker*. Her exquisite performance is credited with turning the then-obscure Tchaikovsky ballet into a holiday classic. After nearly two decades at the heart of American ballet, headlining everything from *Fire Bird* to *Swan Lake*, Maria hung up her toe shoes to teach. She put classical dance on the map in the Windy City, founding the Chicago Ballet with her fellow dancer sister and serving as its first artistic director. Remembered for bringing thrilling energy and individuality to impeccable technique, Maria returned to center stage in her seventies as a Kennedy Center and National Medal of Arts honoree.

"If anything at all, perfection is not when there is nothing to add, but when there is nothing left to take away."

MARIA TALLCHIEF
PRIMA BALLERINA

Kathryn Sullivan

BORN 1951

GEOLOGIST • NAVAL RESERVE OCEANOGRAPHY OFFICER •
FIRST AMERICAN WOMAN TO WALK IN SPACE

Many people dream of going to space. Kathryn Sullivan has done it three times, logging five hundred and thirty-two hours in orbit. As a longtime NASA mission specialist and payload commander, Kathryn has helped open up new worlds and galaxies of knowledge. She deployed the Hubble Space Telescope that allows us to peer into the furthest reaches of the universe. Plus, she gave us profound new insights into the workings of our own tiny corner of the solar system with the launch of NASA's Mission to Planet Earth. Years of planning and training went into these technical feats. Space shuttle crews and their ground control are the ultimate high-performance teams—operating in an environment where the speed, pace, and risk are out-of-this-world. For Kathryn, those "Go for launch" moments of shared life-and-death decision making are her favorite souvenirs as an astronaut. Why? Because the greatest proof of lessons really learned is having the instinctive assurance to respond full tilt to unplanned threats and opportunities.

Even beyond NASA, Kathryn has had a true "explorer's career." She's served in the Navy and earned her private pilot license. Two presidents have tapped her for leadership stints with the National Oceanic and Atmospheric Association, and she spent a decade at the helm of a museum that's at the forefront of hands-on STEM education. Today, the multi-dimensional expert is writing the rule book for how teams maintain those orbiting satellites that keep pushing human horizons.

"I love to witness those kind of really crisp moments of absolute expertise in action."

KATHRYN SULLIVAN
ASTRONAUT

Cathy Lanier

BORN 1967

SINGLE MOM • POLICE CHIEF •
THE NATIONAL FOOTBALL LEAGUE'S TOP DEFENDER

In 2007, at age thirty-nine, Cathy Lanier became the first female chief of police in Washington, D.C. Her rise through the ranks was swift. She signed up for the Academy as a single mom and high-school dropout who wanted to give her son a better life. She went from patrolling the beat to overseeing narcotics and counterterrorism. She bravely battled sexual harassment in the workplace, keeping her head high while earning two grad degrees in national security. When selected to lead the department, Cathy didn't necessarily feel ready for the high-profile gig, but she also didn't blink. She trusted that her commitment and willingness to learn would see her through. They did. Cathy became one of the country's most admired and longest-serving city police chiefs, earning a rep for responsive community policing.

Cathy was heavily recruited during her tenure in law enforcement. She repeatedly declined to leave her post . . . that is, until the National Football League came knocking. Planning for the more than two thousand public events staged each year in the nation's capital—from marches to visits by world leaders—served as the perfect primer for modernizing the NFL's game-day security. The Super Bowl alone requires Cathy to coordinate with forty government agencies; as the most watched event on television, it's accorded the same threat level as a presidential inauguration!

"When your gut instinct is very, very strong, you've got to go with your gut."

CATHY LANIER
SECURITY CHIEF

Tina Fey

BORN 1970

IMPROV ARTIST • SCREENWRITER • ACTOR, PRODUCER,
AUTHOR, PLAYWRIGHT & . . .

Dubbed one of the funniest women in the world today, Tina Fey first broke into the entertainment industry in the Chicago comedy scene. She thrived at improv, that unscripted style of building an in-the-moment story together. It relies on the ensemble being all-in, keenly listening and saying "yes AND" while spontaneously teeing up your teammates. Overthink it, and you leave your fellow actors and audience hanging.

Tina has adopted the same all-in principle when it comes to her career, using her sterling wit and tough work ethic to break new ground for women in the entertainment industry. The shy, nerdy drama student graduated into a formidable triple threat—writer, actor, and producer—with nine Emmys and three Golden Globes to her name. Hired as the first female head writer at *Saturday Night Live*, Tina eventually shifted in front of the camera as an acerbic co-anchor on the show's flagship "Weekend Update." When she delivered the impression of the century as Sarah Palin during the 2008 US presidential election, ratings soared for both *SNL* and *30 Rock*, her critical darling of a sitcom based on her life at NBC. Since then, she has starred in blockbusters and produced quirky TV series, penned a best-selling book, and cohosted fabulously funny award shows alongside her BFF, Amy Poehler. Today, the multi-talented Tina is still going for it with ingeniously offbeat new projects, like translating her go-to teen flick *Mean Girls* into a Broadway musical.

"You can't be that kid standing at the top of the waterslide, overthinking it. You have to go down the chute."

TINA FEY
COMEDIAN

Courtney Banghart

BORN 1978

MULTI-SPORT ATHLETE • CULTURE SHAPER • OPTIMISTIC DREAM BUILDER

Courtney Banghart is a student of leadership, who, in evolving her own philosophy and authentic style, has become heralded alongside the world's great contemporary leaders. She's an athlete who realized that her own passion for sports could translate into a meaningful vocation. Courtney is the winningest coach in Princeton basketball history. Besides earning six Ivy League titles, she led a storied team of Tigers (with no All-Americans) to a perfect 30–0 regular season, securing the best-ever NCAA tournament seed for an Ivy while maintaining high academic standards. It's an achievement that saw her named the 2015 Naismith National Coach of the Year and one of *Fortune Magazine*'s World's 50 Greatest Leaders. How does this relentless leader produce overachieving teams? By approaching each player's progress one-on-one and by not letting the team settle into boundary-imposing roles.

A former Ivy League baller herself, Courtney has lived the scholar/athlete experience and carries forth a "why not us?" mantra when it comes to the dream of busting brackets during March Madness. Still, Courtney never intended to call the plays. The neuroscience undergrad returned to her alma mater as an assistant coach while earning her grad degree. Her thesis: studying the leadership styles of now-legendary coaches, including North Carolina State's Sandra Kay Yow and University of Connecticut's Luigi "Geno" Auriemma. Ultimately, developing lifelong leaders is this coach's true work. Her training unlocks each woman's unique potential to make her future journey count.

"Don't let the parts get lost in the whole."

COURTNEY BANGHART
BASKETBALL COACH

COURAGE & CAUTION

Clarissa "Clara" Barton

1821–1912

TEACHER • ANGEL OF THE BATTLEFIELD • INDEFATIGABLE HUMANITARIAN

Clara Barton never let convention stand in the way of her do-gooding. When she saw "anything new that might improve the past," she went for it. Famous for founding the American branch of the Red Cross, Clara had already cycled through several remarkable careers before she became a pioneer of disaster relief and preparedness. By age fifteen she was a teacher, later opening the first public school in New Jersey. When local authorities sent a male principal to take charge of her six hundred pupils, Clara took her leave and became one of the federal government's earliest female employees as a clerk in the US patent office.

She was thirty-nine when the Civil War broke out. Seeing her former students turned soldiers made her long to be on the frontlines herself. After organizing relief for troops quartered in the nation's Capital, she started personally delivering supplies she had gathered to field hospitals and volunteering as an unofficial nurse. After the war, she set up the Missing Soldiers Office to reunite families before her doctor sent her packing to Europe for some much-needed R&R. Even on vacation, Clara couldn't help but find some new way to be useful. Discovering the International Red Cross gave her a formal framework for her self-organized relief efforts. She established its American wing in 1881, while successfully lobbying for the United States to sign on to the Geneva Convention. The fierce and famous leader of the organization for more than twenty years, Clara opened minds while saving lives.

"It irritates me to be told how things have always been done. I defy the tyranny of precedent. I cannot afford the luxury of a closed mind."

CLARA BARTON
AMERICAN RED CROSS FOUNDER

Bessie Coleman

1892–1926

MANICURIST • FIRST AFRICAN-AMERICAN WOMAN TO EARN A PILOT'S LICENSE • AIR-SHOW STUNT PILOT

Brave Bessie Coleman was a daredevil with a dream: lifting up her race by taking to the skies. When no US flying school would accept her, the manicurist learned French and saved up to study abroad. After becoming the first American to qualify as an aviator at France's most famous flight school, she found work as a test pilot in Europe.

Feted by ace fighter pilots, aviation engineers, and even royalty, Bessie drummed up PR for her triumphant 1923 return to the States. She used it to draw crowds to her air shows, performing stunts for awestruck audiences of all races and doing it with patriotic flair, loop de loops, and parachuting women! Bessie soon bought her own plane . . . then took a nosedive in it in front of ten thousand people. The broken leg and ribs didn't keep her from the cockpit. Instead, she took her act across her native South, putting on exhibitions, films, and lectures (the children she hoped to inspire always got in free). Bessie was on the verge of realizing her dream of opening her own school to train African-American pilots when a test flight threw her to her death. The Bessie Coleman Aero Club honored her memory by taking up her cause. African-American aviators still pay tribute to the trailblazer with an annual flyover of her Chicago gravesite.

"If I can create the minimum of my plans and desires, there shall be no regrets."

BESSIE COLEMAN
AVIATOR

Margaret Mead

1901–1978

NATURAL HISTORY MUSEUM CURATOR • MOTHER OF
CULTURAL ANTHROPOLOGY • STUDENT OF CIVILIZATION

Among the iconic quotations with questionable origins is Margaret Mead's words: "Never doubt that a small group of thoughtful, committed citizens can change the world." Whether or not the leading anthropologist actually said them, they're undoubtedly words that capture her spirit. Margaret famously put a new social science on the map, but she never limited herself to being a detached observer of past and present civilizations. She also used her expertise to step out as a passionate protector of future civilizations, founding an institute to promote understanding across cultures and protesting the nuclear arms race, stumping for children's health, and serving as the inaugural speaker at the very first Earth Day. Offering insights about the haste and waste of American culture, she pushed for cautious, long-view policy making . . . decisions sprung from our "cultivated human hearts," not the quarterly "calculating machine."

Margaret's firsthand observations of remote cultures spurred fresh perspectives on her own. She published more than forty books and some thousand articles on subjects ranging from Bali to her own backyard. Margaret's studious travels taught her that "the way things are" is never a given and reaffirmed her belief that collective hard work could create new and better possibilities.

"We must return to a calm and responsible frame of mind in which we can face the long patient tasks ahead."

MARGARET MEAD
ANTHROPOLOGIST

Maya Lin

BORN 1959

MONUMENT DESIGNER • ENVIRONMENTALIST SCULPTOR •
MEMORIAL INNOVATOR

In 1995, Maya Lin was commissioned to create a memorial for heroic helicopter pilot François-Xavier Bagnoud. Always an artist whose moment of inspiration hatches out of meticulous research, she knew this project called for a deep dive into aerodynamics. The result was *The Wave Field*, an earthen landscape sculpture in Michigan whose grassy ridges evoke the hidden forces behind flight. Understanding that delicate balance of gravity, thrust, lift, and drag reminded Maya that any kind of flying requires resistance.

It's a lesson she learned early in her career after landing her first high-profile gig as an undergrad. When Maya entered a contest to design the Vietnam Veterans Memorial, her proposal was chosen unanimously from over a thousand entries. Yet, people soon questioned her age and inexperience, even her Asian heritage. Accustomed to aggrandizing white stone monuments that were vertical and highly ornamented, many argued her minimalist vision—a mirrorlike wall of polished black granite—dishonored the dead. Maya's conviction triumphed in spite of pushback. So much so, her work ended up setting the new standard for public monuments as the Vietnam Veterans Memorial became a national shrine attracting millions of visitors each year. Since then, Maya has continued to innovate the form with credits that include Alabama's Civil Rights Memorial, Yale's Women's Table, and "What Is Missing?," her own online multi-media "mega project" that's raising awareness about species extinction.

"To fly, we have to have resistance."

MAYA LIN
ARTIST-ARCHITECT

Sallie Krawcheck

BORN 1964

EQUITY RESEARCHER • FINANCIAL SERVICES EXECUTIVE •
WOMEN'S INVESTMENT PLATFORM FOUNDER

As a "serial CEO" and entrepreneur, Sallie Krawcheck knows a lot about building great teams. As a self-proclaimed "financial feminist" who invests in companies leading the way on gender diversity, she's one of the foremost advocates for bringing a mix of voices to the table. For her, that means seeking out people not only with different backgrounds but also different mentalities—from the risk-taker to the sober voice of reason.

Reeling from the hostile climate she encountered as a young investment banker, Sallie almost left the sector until she found her niche as an equity researcher. Her reputation as the "last honest analyst" helped her climb the ladder to head up wealth management for some of the world's most reputable banks. Yet there were very few women alongside her at the top. Sallie made up her mind to close the investment gap. The newly minted entrepreneur took over a women's professional network, transforming it into the global community for economic empowerment, Ellevate. Then, she built Ellevest, a digital investment platform with an algorithm based on new scientific insights about female investors and women-led businesses. Today, Sallie's teams are affording women freedom by encouraging the candid discussions about money that will help them achieve financial control and equality.

"You want the optimist and the pessimist, the go-getter and the jaded one who has seen it all. You need to have all of it."

SALLIE KRAWCHECK

INVESTOR

Leymah Gbowee

BORN 1972

SOCIAL WORKER • NOBEL PEACE PRIZE LAUREATE •
FAITHFUL FOUNDATION FOUNDER

Leymah Gbowee was seventeen when civil war broke out in her native Liberia. Nearly fourteen years of conflict later, she decided that it was time for the country's mothers to put a stop to the violence that had claimed two hundred and fifty thousand of their children. As a trauma counselor who cared for former child soldiers and other victims of war, Leymah had seen it all and gradually become "immune to fear." She used that fearlessness to inspire other women to act. Building a cross-faith coalition of Muslims and Christians, Leymah mobilized thousands for a rolling peace protest. Their pray-ins and nonviolent demonstrations are credited with spurring peace talks and setting the stage for the election of Liberia's first female president, Ellen Johnson Sirleaf.

Leymah wasn't afraid to take bold steps to get there. When talks finally resumed in Ghana, she made tracks. The movement followed, organizing a human barricade to keep both parties at the negotiating table. The protesters only avoided arrest by threatening to shed every piece of clothing—an act that would have cast shame on the security officers. Leymah's timely appeal to a cultural taboo allowed the women to stand their ground until a deal was made. Today, the Nobel laureate is engaging more women in peace and security governance in Africa while continuing to walk boldly on a global stage.

"Leaving large footprints entails not walking on tiptoes."

LEYMAH GBOWEE
PEACE ACTIVIST

OVERCOME & BECOME

Sheila Wellington

BORN 1932

MENTAL HEALTH PROFESSIONAL • THINK TANK EXEC •
MANAGEMENT PROFESSOR

Before Sheila Wellington became one of the foremost advocates for advancing women in business, she spent eighteen years working in mental health facilities. Her background was in public health, but being the director of a state mental hospital taught her plenty about management. Like, "When the going gets tough, the tough get creative." When a budget freeze left her short-staffed, she convinced her team that together they could meet the crisis. In the end, many of the band aids they devised actually led to long-term improvements, including an innovative day-treatment program that became a nationwide model.

When Sheila left the health sector, she remained dedicated to helping people overcome and bounce higher . . . this time, with women in the workplace. After serving as Yale's first female secretary and VP, she was recruited to head up the barrier-breaking nonprofit Catalyst. Over her tenure, Sheila upped the women in corporate leadership by consulting on diversity and inclusion initiatives for companies, providing legal and financial support to members, and undertaking studies that made them the go-to resource for reliable information on the issues. One of Sheila's major research reveals that mentorship is one of the biggest professional advantages men have over women. It's an insight that underlies many of today's thriving women's networks. Because, sometimes, leaning in requires a nudge.

"At the end of the day,
it's not how far you fall but
how high you bounce."

SHEILA WELLINGTON
BUSINESS LEADER

Alice Greenwald

BORN 1952

HISTORIAN OF RELIGION • CURATOR •
OVERSEER OF EXPERIENCES THAT AWAKEN OUR CONSCIENCE

As the founding director of the 9/11 Memorial Museum, Alice Greenwald had a difficult decision to make—how do you create an experience that helps people reckon with such an unthinkable tragedy? Today's museums aren't about elite collections of high cultural artifacts. Instead, curators have become public storytellers. Alice's task was to find a unique way to share a catastrophic, world-changing narrative.

As a veteran of the US Holocaust Memorial Museum, she had a background in designing spaces and programs that allow people to bear witness to the worst of human history while coming away with a deepened understanding of our shared humanity. Alice approached her new project with the same philosophy, mixing unvarnished facts with transcendent symbolism. She oversaw the transformation of the former site of the World Trade Center into a serene, park-like setting with interior exhibits that present startling traces of the 2001 terrorist attack, from massive artifacts like an impacted remnant of the North Tower's steel frame to poignant personal ephemera like homemade missing persons posters. Where the Twin Towers once stood are two meditative acre-size pools that invert the buildings' height with some of the world's largest man-made waterfalls. Today, Alice has become president and CEO of the museum she spent a decade envisioning. Since its 2014 opening, millions have made the journey, confronting the past to imagine a way beyond.

"Bearing witness to the unimaginable is the only way to imagine a way beyond it."

ALICE GREENWALD
MUSEUM DIRECTOR

Ellen DeGeneres

BORN 1958

STREAM-OF-CONSCIOUSNESS STAND-UP •
BARRIER-BREAKING SITCOM STAR • FEEL-GOOD QUEEN OF COMEDY

Ellen DeGeneres first turned to comedy to help see her mom through a tough divorce. At twenty, she relied on humor to heal from her own heartache after her girlfriend died in a car crash. Waiting tables, living in a flea-ridden basement apartment, and still grieving from the sudden loss, Ellen coped by writing her first bit, a hypothetical "phone call to God" to ask the questions that were haunting her. She thought, "Johnny Carson would love this," and came away from the tragedy with a new goal. Several years later, when she was invited to perform on the iconic late-night show, that routine made her the first and only female comic to be called over to his couch for a chat.

After working her way up from a stand-up with her own endearing brand of observational humor to the star of her own sitcom, Ellen almost lost everything in 1997 after she boldly came out as a gay woman on-air. Quickly ousted from the network, it took a few years of waiting for the phone to ring for her courage to be rewarded. Since then, she's made a serious comeback with a thirty-time Emmy-winning talk show, not to mention a starring role in the beloved *Finding Nemo* and a stint as an unconventional *CoverGirl.* In the end, the biggest reward for this dance-loving, prank-playing daytime host is inspiring people around the world to embrace kindness and fearlessly "live their truth."

> "Care. Love. Be outraged. Be devastated. Just don't give up. The world needs good humans today."

ELLEN DEGENERES
TALK SHOW HOST

Tammy Duckworth

BORN 1968

COMBAT PILOT • DISABLED WAR HERO •
FIRST US SENATOR TO GIVE BIRTH WHILE IN OFFICE

In 2004, a rocket-propelled grenade launched by Iraqi insurgents hit the Black Hawk helicopter Tammy Duckworth was piloting. One of her legs was vaporized, the other crushed. But her crew didn't give up on her. They managed to land and pull her from the wreckage. Waking up in a wheelchair with a Purple Heart, Tammy could have been excused for feeling defeated. Instead, she used her remarkable survival and feeling of debt to her fellow soldiers as motivation to fight for the underdogs at home—with lionhearted determination and a wicked sense of humor.

Born in Bangkok to a Thai mother, Tammy had military roots in her US Marine father. She didn't join up herself until she grew chummy with Army folk while earning her PhD in political science in Washington, D.C. When the disabled veteran was invited as an honored guest to the State of the Union address, she found her next calling: politics. In 2016, Tammy was elected as the junior senator from Illinois. The Army's battlefield imperative to "never leave anyone behind" is now her political mantra. As a survivor, she's especially attuned to the human costs of policy making, whether it affects soldiers, veterans, immigrants, women, or the working poor. Today, Tammy stands on titanium prosthetic legs . . . the perfect symbol for expressing her refusal to buckle under pressure.

"I still wake up every morning trying to be worthy of this miraculous second chance."

TAMMY DUCKWORTH
SENATOR

Tarana Burke

BORN 1973

SURVIVOR • NONPROFIT DIRECTOR • #METOO FOUNDER & LEADER

Tarana Burke was serving as a camp director when a thirteen-year-old camper opened up about the abuse she was experiencing at home. Tarana herself had been assaulted by neighborhood boys as a child, but she felt lost for a response, silencing the teen girl with a referral to a counselor. She later realized even an empathetic "me too" would have helped. It led Tarana to foster a group of survivor-activists so that young victims from disadvantaged communities would know that they're not alone.

Eleven years later, when a report broke about harassment allegations surrounding one of Hollywood's top producers, it cracked open a much bigger story about the shocking prevalence of sexual violence. Actress Alyssa Milano encouraged women to come forward with their experiences, marking each testimony with a shared #MeToo. Suddenly, the Bronx-born Tarana, who first coined "Me Too" in 2006 as a way to help fellow survivors heal, found herself at the center of a surging movement. Prior to its going viral, Tarana had always kept the phrase within safe spaces; she never intended for it to become a hashtag. But when twelve million social media posts emerged under that banner, she recognized the power of public testimony to destigmatize survivors' experiences and generate a change-making global conversation. While Tarana and her cause have been drawn into the spotlight on red carpets and magazine covers, her focus is on using this moment to further the movement to end abuse and spread "empowerment through empathy."

"Healing is a lifelong journey and the hardest part is starting."

TARANA BURKE
SURVIVOR-ACTIVIST

Taylor Swift

COUNTRY MUSIC DARLING • TEN-TIME GRAMMY WINNER •
SHAKE-IT-OFF EVANGELIST

"Be true to yourself" is perhaps the most commonly shared advice. Known for bold, in-the-public-eye transformations, Taylor Swift has always stuck to that age-old adage by allowing herself to constantly evolve. Embracing the personal revolutions that come with being an artist, she's gone from driven kid talent–show contestant to romantic, wavy-tressed Nashville sweetheart to edgy platinum pop diva.

The audiences for Taylor's deeply personal songwriting have grown exponentially with her over the course of a record-making career that's been astonishingly record-breaking. In sales (forty million albums). In chart-topping hits (including three number-one singles in one album). Industry awards (more than two hundred wins). And philanthropy (four-time most charitable celeb). The youngest-ever winner of the Grammy's top honors, she also became the first woman to win Album of the Year twice. Then, in 2016, she became the world's highest-paid celeb according to *Forbes*. The brand-savvy artist has pioneered the empowered pop star–CEO role while using her influence to take on tech giants who would trample on musicians' intellectual property rights. Still, Taylor's off-the-charts success has come with intense media scrutiny, plus a raft of critics who don't recognize her talent or leadership creds. Her response to the haters? Lyrics that brilliantly poke fun at her "bad rep" . . . and (dance-inspiring) anti-bullying anthems that have encouraged us all to "shake it off."

"The goal is to continue to change, and never change in the same way twice."

TAYLOR SWIFT

SINGER-SONGWRITER

CONVICTION & COMPROMISE

Susan B. Anthony

1820–1906

ABOLITIONIST • WRITER & NEWSPAPER EDITOR • EQUALITY CRUSADER

This New England schoolteacher's tireless activism in the face of ridicule has made her a timeless feminist icon. Susan B. Anthony teamed up with fellow abolitionist Elizabeth Cady Stanton to spearhead the US women's suffrage movement. Together, the two launched a political organization to push for a federal amendment and published a weekly newspaper under the audacious title *The Revolution*. Susan was regularly taunted as a bitter old maid, criticized in biting editorials and even hung in effigy. She pressed on with daring tactics. In 1872, she was fined a hundred dollars for "illegally" casting a ballot in a general election. Besides refusing to pay, she delivered a public lecture billed as "the invincible Susan B" and speaking on the question "Is it a crime for a citizen of the United States to vote?"

Susan was famous for traveling the country solo with her trademark red shawl and alligator purse, a symbol that women couldn't open their own bank accounts or execute contracts. She stumped for women's and workers' rights, spreading a rallying call that remains relevant today: "Equal pay for equal work!" Fourteen years after her death, the cofounder of the National Women's Suffrage League was honored as the namesake of the Nineteenth Amendment that gave US women the right to vote. She had predicted the victory herself in the steadfast conclusion of her final speech, delivered on her eighty-sixth birthday: "Failure is impossible."

"Forget conventionalisms; forget what the world will say, whether you are in your place or out of your place; think your best thoughts, speak your best words, do your best works."

SUSAN B. ANTHONY
SUFFRAGIST

Drew Gilpin Faust

BORN 1947

CIVIL WAR HISTORIAN • DEPARTMENT CHAIR & DEAN • IVY LEAGUE DOOR-OPENER

At nine years old, Drew Gilpin Faust secretly sent a letter to President Eisenhower sixty miles away in the White House. Writing in all caps, the earnest young activist felt compelled to express her opposition to the segregation and prejudice around her and in a household that maintained a careful silence surrounding race. As she continued her studies, Drew went from civil rights activism to investigation of the root causes of the conflict. Being an effective leader for change, she realized, depended on a deep understanding of your context. The rural Virginia farm girl became a prominent historian of the American South, department head, and dean. Then, in 2007, she was tapped for a defining leadership role: president of Harvard.

Drew was the first woman to hold the top job in the world-famous university's near four-hundred-year history. At first, she bristled at the constant references to her "tokenism," but she's come to see how her visibility as "one of the world's most powerful women" is an inspiration to others. Drew herself was educated at an all-girls academy and college, empowering contexts that surrounded her with academic role models and prepped her to view women as leaders. If she'd gone to Harvard in the 1960s, Drew admits, she probably wouldn't have become its president. She brought that same historian's insight to the role, successfully mobilizing diverse stakeholders by taking time to really listen and understand where they're coming from.

"History, like leadership, is about change, about understanding what makes change happen, about who embraces change and why, and about who resists it and how."

DREW GILPIN FAUST
UNIVERSITY PRESIDENT

Christiana Figueres

BORN 1956

ANTHROPOLOGIST • PUBLIC SERVANT • COLLABORATIVE DIPLOMAT

This mantra powered Christiana Figueres down the tortuous path to sealing the deal on an unprecedented compromise: getting the world's nations to sign on to a plan to protect the one planet that we all share. As executive secretary of the UN Framework Convention on Climate Change, she was the "force of nature" behind the historic 2015 Paris deal. The goal: put the brakes on climate change by cutting back on fossil fuels and carbon emissions. It may have taken six years to broker, but it's the first time in world history that more than a hundred and ninety-five countries have agreed to anything. Throughout the process, Christiana won buy-in by being blunt about the challenges yet unrelenting in her optimism. After all, as she puts it: "I have not met a single person who is motivated by bad news."

The Costa Rican diplomat first became interested in environmental issues when she realized one of the species she loved as a child—the golden toad—had become extinct by the time her daughters were born. Before joining the UN, Christiana founded a nonprofit center to boost sustainable development in Latin America while representing her country as an international negotiator. A longtime collaborator with earth-friendly companies, the green change-maker continues to negotiate concrete actions while restoring hope.

"Impossible is not a fact;
it's an attitude."

CHRISTIANA FIGUERES
CLIMATE CHANGE CHAMPION

Venus Williams

SPORTS PRODIGY • FIRST AFRICAN-AMERICAN WOMAN TO BE NUMBER ONE IN WORLD TENNIS • SERIAL ENTREPRENEUR

Venus Williams is a tennis legend. A seven-time Grand Slam singles winner who's earned five Wimbledon titles. A four-time Olympic gold medalist who's made it to the podium at four different Games. Plus, the all-time record holder for Grand Slams played. She's famous for bringing her style and personality to the court along with her A-game. And Venus is still going strong more than two decades after going pro in spite of having an incurable immune disorder that inflicts constant aches. On the court, she's used to controlling every detail of her performance. When she delved into off-court business, she brought the same unstoppable attitude but quickly learned it was impossible to handle everything herself. In fact, becoming an entrepreneur with thriving athleisure and interior design companies gave Venus a new sense of balance. It's taught her how to collaborate and delegate—and how to say "no." Her biggest founder's advice? Learn how to graciously pass . . . even on big ideas or great opportunities that ultimately aren't the right fit.

No wonder Venus has to prioritize. Besides being a top-ten tennis player and businesswoman, she's also a design student and part owner of the Miami Dolphins. An involved philanthropist, too, she recently teamed with sister Serena to honor their older sister—killed in a drive-by shooting in 2003—by opening a social services center in their Compton, Los Angeles County, hometown.

"Say 'no' with a smile."

VENUS WILLIAMS
PRO TENNIS PLAYER

Tulsi Gabbard

BORN 1981

Congresswoman Tulsi Gabbard opens every speech and meeting with "Aloha"— and not because it means "hello." In her native Hawaii, Aloha has a much deeper resonance, as a guiding spirit of mutual respect. The Polynesian word's profound meaning is so central to their island culture that it's written into state law.

Tulsi has emerged as a fresh face for politics and a youthful presence who is, among other things, an avid surfer, yogi, and vegetarian. But she also brings the gravitas of rich experience—as a onetime local rep, city councilor, and Army major who voluntarily enlisted post-9/11 for two tours of duty in the Middle East. Throughout her career, Tulsi has kept tradition alive by embodying Aloha in action. She lived it as a shy, homeschooled girl who plucked up courage to serve others by running for office. She lived it in the military, especially when tasked with training the initially wary all-male Kuwaiti security forces. And she's living it as a politician who's outspoken on policy matters without resorting to name-calling. Known for working across the aisle and never defaulting to party lines, Tulsi has championed the "Aloha spirit" that has set her apart in the current divisive climate on Capitol Hill. But the rising star is increasingly speaking to a rising tide, eager to focus on what we all share in common to create lasting change.

"When I 'Aloha' you, it means I'm coming to you with an open heart. I'm coming to you with respect, with compassion, and with an understanding that we all stand on equal ground."

TULSI GABBARD
CONGRESSPERSON

Jennifer Lawrence

BORN 1990

DOWN-TO-EARTH A-LISTER • ACADEMY AWARD WINNER • ACTIVIST-ACTOR

Jennifer Lawrence was still looking for her strong suit when a talent agent spotted the Kentucky teen while she was vacationing in New York City. After her first cold read, she knew she'd found her calling. The young natural quickly graduated from TV ads to TV shows to the silver screen. By age twenty-two, she had a Best Actress Oscar under her belt, earning even more admiration for her signature good-humored response after tripping on her way to claim the award. When she snagged one of the most sought-after roles to date—the gutsy girl-hero Katniss Everdeen in *The Hunger Games* franchise—"J-Law" became *The Girl on Fire* in her own right. With her incredible versatility and disarming everygirl demeanor, Jennifer has remained a firm favorite of critics, the press corps, and worldwide audiences.

Jennifer has proven time and again that she's box office gold. But, in 2015, an information hack led to a surprising reveal: that the world's highest-paid actress was still making less than her male costars. It was news to her—and a moment of self-reckoning. The bald truth made her acknowledge a stumbling block in her negotiating stance: being conditioned to worry about coming across as "difficult or spoiled." Since then, Jennifer has given up on altering her manner or requests for the sake of Hollywood execs. She's also joined rank with Hollywood's "leading ladies" to ensure all women are empowered to ask for more.

"I'm over trying to find the 'adorable' way to state my opinion."

JENNIFER LAWRENCE
ACTOR

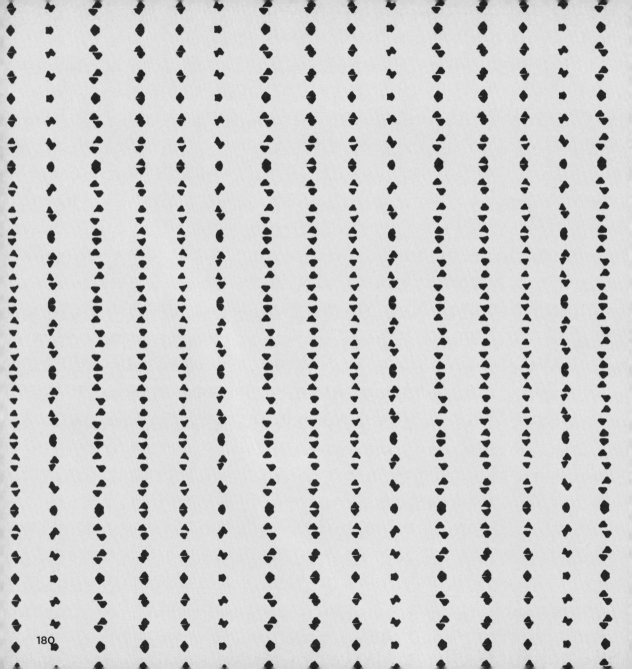

SPEAK UP LISTEN

Marian Anderson

1897–1993

SINGER WITH A HUGE VOCAL RANGE • EQUAL RIGHTS ICON •
A NEW FACE OF THE FIVE DOLLAR BILL

Marian Anderson's 1939 concert at the Lincoln Memorial was a watershed moment in US history. After the Daughters of the American Revolution refused to let the African-American contralto sing at their renowned Constitution Hall, the slight made national headlines. First Lady Eleanor Roosevelt resigned her DAR membership over the incident and helped Marian organize a much bigger concert. On Easter Day, Marian took the mic before an audience of seventy-five thousand on the National Mall. The defiant performance established her as a founding mother of the civil rights movement.

Marian first started singing with her church choir, teaching herself piano to be her own accompanist. Her congregation so admired her talent and commitment that they raised five hundred dollars for her to study with a voice teacher. Even though she is now considered one of the greatest vocalists of the twentieth century, Marian's pro career got off to a shaky start. Attendance at her first 1924 recital was poor and so were the reviews. But Marian struck a chord when she bravely entered a competition sponsored by the New York Philharmonic the following year. Her first-place finish set her up as an in-demand classical singer, one who used her voice to create a path to equality. She toured Europe and sang at Carnegie Hall, was invited to the White House and delivered the anthem at a presidential inauguration. In 1963, Marian gave a powerful reprisal of her first triumph at the Lincoln Memorial for Martin Luther King's March on Washington.

"The minute a person whose words mean a great deal takes the open-hearted and courageous way, many others follow."

MARIAN ANDERSON
OPERA SINGER

Madeleine Albright

BORN 1937

LATE BLOOMER • DIPLOMAT & PROFESSOR • MASTER OF NONVERBAL COMMUNICATION

Madeleine Albright got her career-defining job at a time when most people would be thinking about retiring. In 1997, at nearly sixty, she became the United States' first female secretary of state. She's also the only immigrant besides Henry Kissinger to have held the top cabinet seat. Madeleine came to the States as a political refugee whose family had fled Nazi-occupied Czechoslovakia (later, she would learn that her grandparents were Holocaust victims). Her wartime upbringing gave her a profound appreciation for liberty and democracy; her diplomat dad got her hooked on politics. But between supporting her husband's career, raising her daughters, and completing her studies, Madeleine took a long time to get her foot in the door.

As soon as she did, she became a force to be reckoned with as a trusted advisor, beloved professor, and game-changing diplomat. During her four years as the United States' top diplomat, Madeleine turned her notoriety as a token woman into a strength for fostering dialogue and personal relationships. Her favorite "fashion statement"? Breaking the ice with "pin diplomacy"—sending witty and powerful messages simply by wearing the right brooch. Think: a snake after she was called an "unparalleled serpent," a beetle after conference rooms were bugged. The original Madam Secretary continues to be a pathfinder for female leaders and a major player in political debates. It may have taken her a while to find her voice, but she's "not going to be quiet now."

"We should use our opinions to start discussions, not to end them."

MADELEINE ALBRIGHT
SECRETARY OF STATE

Susan Cain

BORN 1968

LAWYER • RESEARCHER & AUTHOR • QUIET EVANGELIST

Susan Cain rose to fame by giving a voice to introverts. Her advocacy for the quiet power of introverts as leaders and innovators spoke volumes to a silent majority and unraveled the accepted wisdom of a culture that tends to glorify its gregarious extroverts.

Often surprised by her successes as a corporate lawyer, Susan learned to see the significant advantages of her soft-and-silent side. Like, genuine relationship building that goes beyond superficial networking and leadership based on sincerity, trust, and listening rather than on larger-than-life personalities. She quit her law career and took seven years to write *Quiet* to help other introverts realize their potential. Mustering the courage to take her message to the TED stage, Susan gave a talk that has become one of the most popular of all time. Since then, she's had to do the work of a "pretend extrovert" as a celebrated thought leader. In 2014, she founded the Quiet Revolution to organize the massive community mobilized by her insights. She's teamed with psychologists, technologists, and industrial designers to put her research into practice in homes, schools, and workplaces. Her forceful yet gentle messages for both louder and softer types? Stay true to your temperament. And, tuning in to each person's unique strengths allows everyone to thrive.

"Everyone shines, given the right lighting. For some, it's a Broadway spotlight, for others, a lamplit desk."

SUSAN CAIN
ADVOCATE FOR INTROVERTS

Kinari Webb

BORN 1974

NONPROFIT FOUNDER • "DOCTOR WHO WORKS ON THE
HEALTH OF THE PLANET" • RADICAL LISTENER

Kinari Webb set out to become the next Jane Goodall. Instead, her time studying orangutans in Borneo gave rise to a novel field: international medicine to help heal primates' (and humans') endangered habitat. The Indonesian rainforest was being devastated by illegal logging, primarily by locals. Kinari wanted to help protect this precious ecosystem but knew, as an outsider, that she didn't have all the answers. After training as an MD, she teamed with a US ecologist and an Indonesian dentist to found Health in Harmony. Their innovative approach to conservation kicked off with "radical listening." Why radical? Because they not only heard the affected communities out, but they did so with the intention of turning the input into immediate action.

Kinari and her cofounders went directly to villages and asked what they needed to stop deforestation. The stories were telling—like having to cut sixty trees to pay for a C-section. No one wanted to have to make the impossible choice between their family's immediate well-being and the planet's long-term health. After four hundred hours of listening, the answers were loud and clear: villagers needed access to affordable health care and training in organic farming. Health in Harmony brought over agriculture experts from a nearby island and set up quality clinics where families could pay in any form of non-tree currency, from handicrafts to manure. Their efforts have saved thousands of acres while empowering villagers as problem solvers.

"Compassion matters. It starts with you, it spreads to those around you, and then to the whole planet."

KINARI WEBB
DOCTOR-ECOLOGIST

Amani Al-Khatahtbeh

BORN 1982

BLOGGER • MUSLIM GIRL COMMUNITY CATALYST •
CHAMPION FOR SELF-REPRESENTATION

Amani Al-Khatahtbeh is a Jersey girl. But, as a Muslim living in the post-9/11 United States, she didn't always feel welcome at home. When she was thirteen, her family temporarily relocated to Jordan. Having experienced Islam for the first time in a country where it's common practice, Amani developed a newfound pride in her religion. She returned to the States ready to challenge stereotypes and misconceptions surrounding her community. The teenager began to wear a hijab to own her identity and launched a blog for unapologetic Muslim girls like herself. It quickly became a millennial startup story, evolving from a side-hustle to a worldwide network of authors who are building their own media empire. Today, Amani's platform is creating a space for women to reclaim control over their own narratives. How? By empowering them to represent themselves and by making sure they're seen and heard.

Recently, the *Muslim Girl* book author expanded that mission from first-person writing to self-portraits. Frustrated with the stock woman-clad-in-black-burqa pictures that dominate search results, she partnered with Getty Images to create alternatives: a new archive of photos of Islamic women by Islamic women. Amani is also using her mic to promote cross-cultural understanding by helping the world recognize her community for what it is: an incredibly diverse set of modern women.

"One of the most important things for us to do to amplify voices is to pass the mic . . . If there's someone that can speak to a lived experience that you cannot, do not take up that space, do not speak on their behalf, let them speak for themselves."

AMANI AL-KHATAHTBEH
MEDIA FOUNDER

Mirga Gražinytė-Tyla

BORN 1986

YOUNG MUSIC LOVER • MILLENNIAL MAESTRO • FIRST FEMALE CONDUCTOR OF THE CITY OF BIRMINGHAM SYMPHONY ORCHESTRA

This rising star of the classical music scene is the ultimate nonverbal communicator. It's a form of leading that Mirga Gražinytė-Tyla finds addictive. And powerful. The newest conductor of the world-class City of Birmingham Symphony Orchestra is famous for her dynamic combination of poise and exuberance. A devoted scholar of the diverse music that her group performs, Mirga channels her understanding of a piece into her being and lets it carry the orchestra and audience away. The average leader may not be able to do much with a baton, but we all can take a cue from Mirga's ability to pay attention to the unspoken, coordinate mind and body, and be intensely present.

Mirga grew up in a musical home, but her choirmaster and pianist parents had no interest in her carrying on the family line. Nevertheless, she knew music was her calling, especially when witnessing the power of song to unite her fellow Lithuanians in the wake of the country's collapsed Soviet regime. The world discovered Mirga when she graduated from rigorous training to win international conducting contests. She quickly became a sought-after guest conductor, from LA to Vienna, before her consistent "wow" factor landed her a historic permanent gig. "Tyla" is a recent addition to Mirga's surname. The Lithuanian word for "silence," Tyla is a seemingly counterintuitive choice for a conductor. Yet she believes stillness is the necessary counterpoint to surround sound, in concert and in life.

"It is not necessary at all to use words in order to communicate."

MIRGA GRAŽINYTĖ-TYLA
CONDUCTOR

SUBSTANCE & STYLE

Diana Vreeland

1903–1989

SOCIETY GIRL • GLOBAL TASTEMAKER • FEARED AND ADORED ICON

Outlandish. Eccentric. Extravagant. Unforgettable. Diana Vreeland was a thorough original whose flamboyant style has become the stuff of fashion lore. Dismissed as the ugly duckling of her affluent family, the Paris-born Diana embraced her differences as distinctions, encouraging others to stand out in ways that went beyond conventional beauty. When in 1936 the editor of *Harper's Bazaar* bumped into Diana on the rooftop of a New York nightclub, she was so impressed with the socialite's personal flair that she offered her a job. The chance journalist immediately earned a following with her irreverent "Why Don't You?" column that offered seldom-followed advice . . . like wearing "fruit hats" with currants and cherries or washing your baby's hair with "dead Champagne." With a special knack for being ahead of the trend, Diana popularized everything from bikinis to blue jeans.

As an editor, she was a demanding yet emboldening leader. Incessantly creative, Diana wasn't afraid to "give ideas away" because a new brainchild always followed close on the previous one's footsteps. Her vision often led to lavish and over-budget spreads but never much enriched her personal bank account. After twenty-six years at *Harper's Bazaar*, Diana finally received a $1K raise on her $18K salary. Soon after, *Vogue* poached her. The editor in chief's favorite legacy? Putting the Met's Costume Institute on the map, with fashion exhibits that sidestepped academics to display Diana's own inventive, "lived it" sense of history.

"Style—all who have it share one thing: originality."

DIANA VREELAND
FASHION EDITOR

Sandra Day O'Connor

BORN 1930

PIONEERING LAWYER & POLITICIAN •
LAW SCHOOL NAMESAKE • CIVIC ENGAGER

Sandra Day O'Connor was raised, alongside cowboy companions, on an Arizona ranch with no electricity or running water. Sent away to live with her grandma and get a proper schooling, Sandra brought the rancher spirit with her. She worked hard to be excellent down to the last detail, whether learning obscure statutes or perfecting her golf swing. When her gender left her jobless after law school (in spite of graduating third in her Stanford class), Sandra convinced a county attorney to give her unpaid work. She quickly became his trusted deputy. When a sudden vacancy in the Arizona State Senate gave her an opening, she rolled it into a historic career in government, winning two reelections before becoming a county and state judge.

In 1981, Sandra's grit paid off with her appointment to a ceiling-shattering role: the US Supreme Court's first female justice. Tough but fair in her approach, Sandra often cast the deciding vote and wasn't afraid to grill lawyers whose prep work was not up to snuff when the nation's foundation was at stake. After twenty-four years defending the Constitution, she stepped down. But Sandra's retirement has been anything but retiring. She's become a prominent advocate for judicial independence who's leading a movement to promote civic education so that young students learn to appreciate the government's fine system of checks and balances.

"The first step in getting power is to become visible to others, and then to put on an impressive show."

SANDRA DAY O'CONNOR
SUPREME COURT JUSTICE

Alice Waters

BORN 1944

REFORMED "PICKY EATER" • REVOLUTIONARY RESTAURATEUR • FOOD ACTIVIST

Alice Waters's training as a Montessori teacher in the 1960s prompted her to reimagine what cooking could do—in restaurants and schools, from private homes to global economies. Alice's takeaway from the Montessori classroom was its emphasis on educating and empowering all five of our senses, on making things so (mouthwateringly) appealing that we cannot wait to explore them. She also knew that spending time to carefully cultivate pleasurable spaces and experiences—from the inviting, herb-festooned entrance to Chez Panisse to the brimming displays of vibrantly colorful local produce in her Edible Schoolyard—makes people feel special.

Making things beautiful expresses care. It's also a hopeful catalyst for change. When Alice went to France in college, it opened her eyes to the fine aesthetics of preparing, serving, and savoring food. She borrowed money from her father to open a Berkeley bistro, then realized she needed to establish her own farm to responsibly source the seasonal ingredients that were the basis of her spontaneous menus. Chez Panisse became the model for the farm-to-table revolution—a proven example of culinary sustainability that set the stage for the organic and locavore movements. Today, Alice has gone from head chef to chief evangelist for "slow food values in a fast food culture." An acclaimed innovator, Alice prefers to think of herself as the protector of age-old wisdom, especially celebrating the harvest.

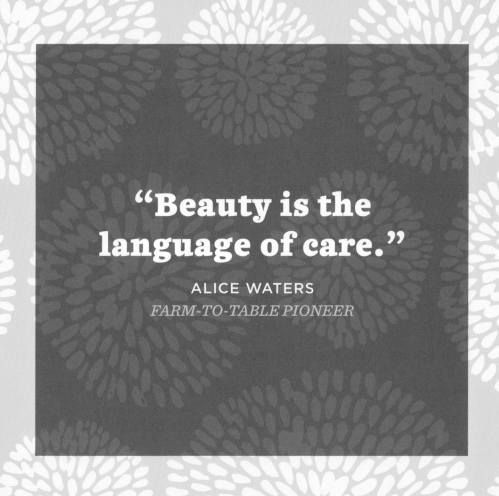

"Beauty is the language of care."

ALICE WATERS
FARM-TO-TABLE PIONEER

Ava DuVernay

BORN 1972

ENTERTAINMENT PR FIRM OWNER • FILM PRODUCER & DISTRIBUTOR •
MIDLIFE CAREER CHANGER

Ava DuVernay had carved out a career running publicity in the film industry. Spending time on sets, she slowly realized: she didn't want to just promote stories; she also wanted to tell them, especially the ones that rarely get greenlighted in Hollywood. Ava decided to give filmmaking a try, starting with a 2008 documentary about her local hip-hop scene. From there, the promising auteur wrote, directed, and figured out how to produce two indie films starring young African-American women . . . both on shoestring budgets that included her own life's savings. *Middle of Nowhere* earned her a nod as best director at the Sundance Festival. Still, Ava didn't quit her day job. Her big break came with the 2014 MLK biopic *Selma.* One of her indie actors, David Oyelowo, was cast as the lead. He convinced the production company to take a chance on Ava. Their gamble paid off with acclaim.

Ava's focus on tapping into the magnificence of her own community and "Black Girl Magic" made mainstream culture pay attention. With her next project, she's become the first African-American woman to direct a film with a budget topping a hundred million. We have a feeling she's headed for more "firsts." She thinks her story has a simple moral for today's artists: don't wait for permission.

"Embedded in the everyday is a magnificence that is so easy to miss because we're so mired in the struggle and what society says we are."

AVA DUVERNAY
DIRECTOR

Amal Clooney

BORN 1978

INTERNATIONAL CRIMINAL LAWYER •
LAW PROFESSOR • STATEMENT-MAKING COVER GIRL

When, on her way to the courthouse, Amal Clooney was hounded by a tabloid journalist asking which designer label she was wearing, her quick-witted response was, "Ede & Ravenscroft" . . . the company that designs the sober black robes sported by British barristers. Amal is a dazzlingly stylish celeb who rocketed to fame with her marriage to notorious Hollywood bachelor George Clooney. But, long before that, she had fashioned a career that took her around the globe as a big-league attorney on high-profile cases. Having the paparazzi trail you to a trial isn't ideal, but Amal acknowledges that, even in her profession, fame has its advantages. However, to make that publicity count, you must have something worth publicizing: a sound case with a righteous cause.

Amal's high-vis status is helping human rights issues make headlines. Born in Lebanon on the brink of civil war, Amal and her family escaped the conflict to settle in the UK. Today, the lawyer is playing a central role in resolving international conflicts, with a client list that includes major players like WikiLeaks' Julian Assange, the ousted president of the Maldives, and former UN Secretary-General Kofi Annan. But Amal's most important clients—like Iraq's little-known Yazidi community, devastated by Islamic State fighters—aren't the familiar names. They're people whose voices might otherwise go unheard without her shining a light on them.

"If you don't have a good case and you don't have a good message, then shining a light on it is not going to get you very far."

AMAL CLOONEY
HUMAN RIGHTS ATTORNEY

Matika Wilbur

BORN 1984

HIGH SCHOOL TEACHER • VISUAL STORYTELLER • JOURNEYING SOCIAL DOCUMENTARIAN

Budding photographer Matika Wilbur was traveling through South America chronicling indigenous peoples when her ancestors called her back home. Matika's great-grandmother came to her in a dream, mentioning it was time to turn her camera toward her own people. That late-night visitation was the start of a wildly ambitious project—to document today's Native Americans via photos that tell the overlooked stories and honor the traditions of tribal people. Matika dubbed it "Project 562" after the number of federally recognized tribes. She's been living her vision ever since. Raising funds with a 2012 Kickstarter campaign, she sold all her possessions to travel the country in an RV, meeting an incredible variety of welcoming strangers turned supporters, from canoe families in her own northwestern Tulalip tribe to Miccosukee elders in the Everglades. Along the way, her work has garnered thousands of backers who've joined in Matika's journey.

Matika's unprecedented photo and oral history brainchild is more than just a record. It's an artistic intervention. Her entrancing exhibitions and educational resources are transforming views of Indian Country, replacing one-dimensional "leathered and feathered" stereotypes with real twenty-first-century Natives. She's also consciously reshaping her community's self-image by uncovering positive indigenous role models. What's Matika ultimately pointing-and-shooting for? Altering perceptions to change the way we treat each other.

"**Perception matters.
Our perception
determines the way
we treat each other.**"

MATIKA WILBUR
PHOTOGRAPHER

GET IT DONE UNPLUG

JANE ADDAMS

1860–1935

CATALYST FOR THE SETTLEMENT HOUSE MOVEMENT •
NOBEL PEACE PRIZE LAUREATE •
PUBLIC PHILOSOPHER & MOTHER OF SOCIAL WORK

Jane Addams is one of history's biggest influencers. The daughter of an affluent Illinois politician chummy with Abe Lincoln, Jane was raised to make a difference. At twenty-seven, she found inspiration in a settlement house serving London's poor communities. Jane decided to bring the social work movement to the United States, cofounding Chicago's Hull House in 1889 to improve the lives of the city's mostly immigrant industrial workers. Her home became a global platform for an enormously wide-ranging program of social reform. She helped institute the juvenile court system and successfully lobbied for child labor laws. She campaigned for public health, women's suffrage, and workers' rights. She headed up the Women's International League for Peace and Freedom and had a hand in building prominent organizations, from the ACLU to the NAACP. She even took a gig as a garbage inspector to promote public sanitation.

One of Jane's lesser-known creds? Sports and rec pioneer. When she first opened Hull House, she started with classrooms and clinics, but her very first addition was an art gallery . . . soon followed by a gymnasium, swimming pool, library, studio spaces, and more. Jane knew play had a profound purpose. Fun, wholesome activities and lively public spaces fostered connections between diverse communities and kindled a creative civic spirit. Besides popularizing the modern urban playground, Jane brought people together with sports, marching bands, seasonal festivals, and unity-sparking public holidays.

"Imaginative powers, the sense
that life possesses variety and color,
are realized most easily in moments of
pleasure and recreation."

JANE ADDAMS
SOCIAL REFORMER

JUNKO TABEI

1939–2016

SCIENCE JOURNAL EDITOR • "CRAZY MOUNTAIN LADY" •
THE ULTIMATE RECREATIONAL CLIMBER

Junko Tabei was a petite four-foot-nine, but she reached extraordinary heights in the world of climbing. She was the first woman (or, as she put it, "the thirty-sixth person") to summit Everest. Also, the first woman to complete the "Seven Summits" circuit by climbing the tallest mountain on each continent. While her Japanese culture tends toward stoicism, the perennial expedition leader quickly discovered that a successful climb (and sometimes your life itself) depended on being constantly communicative about your mental and physical challenges. Ultimately, success came from learning to go at your own pace.

Junko got her first taste of mountaineering as a scrawny ten-year-old school kid and felt an instant affinity. As a sport, it was demanding, but not in a competitive way. She joined a men's climbing group in college, eventually forming her own women's organization. When they set out to climb Everest in 1975, potential sponsors repeatedly told them they should be raising kids, not running around the Himalayas. When they did find backers, it generated an uncomfortable fanfare of publicity around their ascent. From that day forward, Junko decided to never again accept sponsorship, so that each summit (she eventually set the goal of climbing the tallest peak in the world) would be for her alone. According to her philosophy, climbing the mountain is its own reward.

"Even if you go slow, you can make it to the top."

JUNKO TABEI
MOUNTAINEER

ANNE-MARIE SLAUGHTER

BORN 1958

PUBLIC AND INTERNATIONAL AFFAIRS PROF • THINK TANK EXEC • REBOOTER OF THE WORK-LIFE DEBATE

In 2012, Anne-Marie Slaughter wrote an editorial that quickly went viral. She had just left a high-profile post for the US State Department so that she could spend more time with her two young sons. Her reflection on the tough decision that had split her heart and gut—"Why Women Still Can't Have It All"—became *The Atlantic's* most-read article. It also sparked a national conversation about gender equality and work-life balance. But the deeper Anne-Marie got into that dialogue, the more she realized that practically no one can have it all. Today, she's changed her target from an unattainable personal "balance" to the unfinished business of social "equality," lobbying for a society in which the labors of love that keep us all going are valued as much as our professional work.

A longtime academic who's taught international relations in the United States' top law schools, Anne-Marie was suddenly an in-demand authority on work and family issues. She decided to run with it. She wrote a popular book on the subject and became the head of a nonprofit think tank where she could directly influence policy on work, family, and foreign affairs. She may be an admired leader, but she believes her role as an everyday "carer" is just as important. For Anne-Marie, that not only means helping others thrive but also standing up for play, R&R, and vital self-care.

"Care is as important as career."

ANNE-MARIE SLAUGHTER
POLITICAL SCIENTIST

ELIZABETH GILBERT

BORN 1969

MAGAZINE WRITER • TWO-TIME MOVIE MUSE • JOURNEY-INSPIRING MEMOIRIST

After her first marriage ended in a tough divorce, Elizabeth Gilbert picked up the pieces by dropping everything. She left the bustle of New York for a year-long sojourn to Italy, India, and Indonesia. It was a conscious choice to make space for contemplating life and reclaiming genuine pleasure in the living of it . . . from taking lazy naps in sun-drenched gardens to indulging in Roma's most mind-altering luscious gelato to inviting chance meetings with local characters, fellow travelers, and would-be soul mates. Her record of that personal journey to search for fresh joy and meaning led to a memoir. *Eat, Pray, Love* has gone beyond beloved best seller and blockbuster movie to become a cultural touchstone and emboldening handbook that enables women to emerge stronger from spiritual crises.

Even before her breakthrough book, Elizabeth had long found her muse through her travels. At the beginning of her writing career, she spent several years as a wayfaring freelancer, collecting fiction-inspiring experiences as she traversed the States to moonlight at bars, diners, and ranches. Her stint at an infamous saloon in NYC's Lower East Side even became the basis for the smash hit rom-com *Coyote Ugly*. Today, Elizabeth is back on the book circuit with a new font of inspiration. The author known for her wit, warmth, and honesty is on a mission to unlock the world's "Big Magic" . . . so that we can all fearlessly live life creatively.

"Is it so awful to travel through time with no greater ambition than to find the next lovely meal?"

ELIZABETH GILBERT
AUTHOR

MAYA RUDOLPH

BORN 1975

INDIE BAND MEMBER • ACTOR • IN-THE-MOMENT ARTISTE

Maya Rudolph used to fake stomachaches so that she could stay up late and watch *Saturday Night Live*. But with a famous soul singer mom and a music producer dad, it's not surprising that her first foray onto the national stage was with a band. The keyboardist soon returned to her instinct for laugh-making. She cut her teeth with an LA improv troupe before getting her call-up to the sketch comedy big leagues. In 2000, she became a *Saturday Night Live* regular, applauded for her priceless impersonations of everyone from Condoleezza Rice to Paris Hilton.

Her childhood dream had become her life . . . her whole life. But when Maya's first of four children came along, suddenly *SNL* became number two. The six-days-a-week, all-hours grind wasn't meshing with her desire to be present as both a performer and a mom. She stepped away from her former all-consuming passion, and things opened up. Since then, she's fronted films, voiced characters, and done scene-stealing cameos. She's also collaborated on inspired projects with her mega-talented crew, including everything from playing the bride in the blockbuster *Bridesmaids* to covering Prince songs as one half of the tribute band Princess. You can find Maya on every size screen, but don't look for her on social media—she'd rather save her one-liners for work. The comedic genius now knows that being "on" requires being able to turn "off."

"Soak it in. Don't take a picture. Enjoy it right this second."

MAYA RUDOLPH
COMEDIAN

ERIN BENZAKEIN

BORN 1980

WRITER, TEACHER & RESEARCHER • SOCIAL MEDIA SENSATION •
GARDEN INDUSTRY DISRUPTOR

Erin Benzakein grew up spending summers at her great-grandmother's country home. As a little girl, she was chief flower-picker, arranging day-brightening nosegays for her grandma's bedside table. When, years later, Erin found herself an "antsy" young mom in the city, she opted to uproot her family and reconnect with nature. They moved to a small Skagit Valley farm, where Erin started her personal flower garden with rows of her grammy's favorite sweet peas. Her green thumb and bouquets quickly created a local buzz. Suddenly she had pioneered a new profession: farmer-florist.

Erin's eye-catching blooms and arrangements gave her a start, but the business really took off when she started putting a face on the flowers. The self-taught photographer and stylist invested in sharing her own story of life on the farm plus generously passing along her know-how. Floret soon grew an international following. As the company blossomed, Erin wondered how to preserve her original intention: a simpler, more creative lifestyle for her family. Instead of expanding the farm, she decided to sow its seeds . . . with floral workshops, a collective for like-minded local seasonal growers, and a home gardening line. Her two acres are now a high-yield research and education farm that specializes in unusual and heirloom flowers. Today, Erin is inspiring others to follow trails of curiosity while taking time to cultivate beauty in their daily lives.

"If you don't make space for creativity to grow and thrive, it will get stomped out by all the to-dos."

ERIN BENZAKEIN
FARMER-FLORIST

Source It!

DEDICATION & INTRODUCTION

Tapper, Alice Paul. "I'm 10. And I Want Girls to Raise Their Hands." *The New York Times*, October 31, 2017.

GRIT & GRACE

Curie, Marie. Quoted in "Need We Fear Our Nuclear Future?" Lecture by Glenn Seaborg. Maria Sklodowska-Curie Centenary Symposium, October 19, 1967.

Graham, Katherine. "The Power That Didn't Corrupt." Profile by Jane Howard. *Ms. Magazine*, October 1974.

King, Coretta Scott. Martin Luther King Lectureship inaugural address. Wesley Theological Seminary, March 11, 1970.

Albright, Tenley. Achiever interview. The Academy of Achievement, June 21, 1991. http://www.achievement.org/achiever/tenley-albright-m-d/#interview.

Marcario, Rose. "How Patagonia Grows Every Time It Amplifies Its Social Mission." Profile by Jeff Beer. Fast Company, February 21, 2018.

Markle, Meghan. "With Fame Comes Opportunity, But Also a Responsibility." *Elle* UK, November 8, 2016.

PURPOSE & CHANCE

Didrikson Zaharias, Babe. Championship Golf. A.S. Barnes and Company, 1948.

Shriver, Eunice Kennedy. Minerva Awards acceptance speech. The Women's Conference, October 23, 2007. https://www.youtube.com/watch?v=UJpcXHYX4v4.

Kidd, Sue Monk. Commencement address. Scripps College, May 16, 2010.

Kim, Sung Joo. "Living by My Motto: Succeed to Serve." *HuffPost*, July 31, 2014. https://www.huffingtonpost.com/sungjoo-kim/living-by-my-motto-succee_b_5638931.html.

Millman, Debbie. *Look Both Ways*. How Books, 2009.

Wojcicki, Susan. Commencement Address. Johns Hopkins University, May 22, 2014.

HEART & MIND

Kent, Corita, and Jan Stewart. *Learning by Heart*. Bantam Books, 1992.

Goodall, Jane. "Being with Jane Goodall." NOVA's Secret Life of Scientists and Engineers, September 2, 2014. https://www.youtube.com/watch?v=0Qu7Wn1mRYA.

Roddick, Anita. *Body and Soul*. Crown Publications, 1991.

Roberts, Robin, and Veronica Chambers. *Everybody's Got Something*. Grand Central Publishing, 2014.

Cutler, Elizabeth, and Julie Rice. "SoulCycle Founders on Learning to Delegate and Becoming Leaders." Video interview. Fast Company, January 15, 2014. https://www.fastcompany.com/3023549/soul-cycle-founders-on-learning-to-delegate-and-becoming-leaders.

Popova, Maria. "Happy Birthday, Brain Pickings: 7 Things I Learned in 7 Years of Reading, Writing, and Living." *Brain Pickings*, October 23, 2013. https://www.brainpickings.org/2013/10/23/7-lessons-from-7-years.

CONFIDENT & HUMBLE

McDaniel, Hattie. Interview with *The Denver Post*, April 1941. Quoted in *Hattie McDaniel: Black Ambition, White Hollywood* by Jill Watts. HarperCollins, 2005.

Carcaño, Minerva. "Bishop Minerva Carcaño Has a Nearly Impossible Job." Interview by Mary

Hunt. Religion Dispatches, February 24, 2012.

Cassidy, Judaline. "Judaline Cassidy, Plumber & Tradeswoman Activist." MAKERS, September 14, 2017. https://www.makers.com/profiles/59b988735bf623224062bb21.

Witherspoon, Reese. Acceptance speech. *Glamour* Women of the Year Awards, November 9, 2015. https://www.glamour.com/story/reese-witherspoon-women-of-the-year-speech.

Tanamachi, Dana. "Dana Tanamachi: Designer/Illustrator/Typographer." Interview by Tina Essmaker. *The Great Discontent*, March 20, 2012.

Weisberg, Danielle, and Carly Zakin. "Billy, Don't Be a Hero: Our Top Meltdowns." *theSkimm* Blog, November 16, 2017. https://blog.theskimm.com/billy-dont-be-a-hero-our-top-meltdowns-45b55cdea484.

COMMUNITY & SELF

Huerta, Dolores. *A Dolores Huerta Reader*. Edited by Mario T. Garcia. University of New Mexico Press, 2008, p. 33.

Cher. Quoted in "The Off-Screen Chaplin." Review by Jeanine Basinger. *The New York Times*, July 28, 1996.

Smith, Megan. "Passion, Adventure and Heroic Engineering." Keynote address. The Grace Hopper Celebration of Women in Computing, October 3, 2013.

Holmes, Kelly. *Just Go for It!* Hay House Publishers, 2011.

Jackley, Jessica. Commencement address. UCLA, June 15, 2012. https://www.youtube.com/watch?v=sxFQ_38NBwI

Franke, Natalie (@nataliefrank). Social media post. Instagram, December 31, 2017. https://www.instagram.com/p/BdXw8vdHpOA/?hl=en&taken-by=nataliefranke.

WANDER & WONDER

Bird, Isabella. *A Lady's Life in the Rocky Mountains*. G.P. Putnam's Sons, 1879.

Rubin, Vera (@rubin_vera). Social media post. Twitter, February 4, 2016. https://qz.com/873005/vera-rubin-quotes-wisdom-from-a-groundbreaking-astronomer-and-working-mother.

Rivera, Chita. "Chita Rivera on Touring, and Staying Political, at Age 84." Interview by Margaret Gray. *LA Times*, February 6, 2017.

Nye, Naomi Shihab. Interview with Contemporary Authors, 2002. Quoted in *Poetry Foundation* profile, 2010. https://www.poetryfoundation.org/poets/naomi-shihab-nye.

Lutoff-Perlo, Lisa. "How Celebrity Cruises Finally Got Its First Woman Captain." *Fortune* Video, November 30, 2016. fortune.com/video/2016/11/30/elebrity-cruises-finally-got-its-first-woman-capitan.

McCue, Kate. "Five Minutes with Captain Kate McCue." Interview by Joseph Keefe. Maritime Professional, 3Q 2015.

IMAGINE & DO

Potter, Beatrix. Journal entry, November 17, 1896. *The Journal of Beatrix Potter from 1881 to 1897*. Transcribed by Leslie Linder. Frederick Warne & Co. Inc., 1966.

Rice, Condoleezza. Remarks. NFL Women's Summit, February 4, 2016.

Cross, Beth. "You Cannot Delegate Vision." Interview. Insights by Stanford Graduate School of Business, November 2, 2012. https://www.gsb.stanford.edu/insights/you-cannot-delegate-vision.

Bauer, Jeni Britton. "Let's go FORWARD AMERICA." Jeni's Splendid Ice Creams Blog, January 20, 2017. https://jenis.com/blog/lets-go-forward-america.

Duno, Milka. "Female Racer's Lessons from Life in the Fast Lane." Interview by Felicia Taylor. CNN International Edition, June 15, 2012. https://edition.cnn.com/2012/06/15/living/milka-duno-racecar-driver/index.html.

Ulmer, Mikaila. "3 Lessons a 12-Year-Old CEO Learned Building a Business That Got Her to 'Shark Tank.'" Interview by Catherine Clifford. CNBC, January 12, 2017. https://www.cnbc.com/2017/01/12/3-lessons-from-the-12-year-old-ceo-on-shark-tank.html.

TRADITION & INNOVATION

Farmer, Fannie. *The Boston Cooking-School Cookbook*. Little, Brown, and Company, 1896.

Tu, Youyou. "Tu Youyou Becomes First Chinese Woman to Win a Nobel Prize." Interview with CCTV. ITV News, October 12, 2015. https://www.youtube.com/watch?v=S0_SbojHGeo.

Wang, Vera. Interview. Quoted in *Vera Wang* by Anne M. Todd. Chelsea House Publishing, 2007.

Barra, Mary. Commencement address. Kettering University, June 8, 2013. https://www.youtube.com/watch?v=jOokPTtXZYQ.

Kopp, Wendy. Interview. The Academy of Achievement, September 17, 2013. http://www.achievement.org/achiever/wendy-kopp/#interview.

Howard, Ayana. "Being Different Helped a NASA Roboticist Achieve Her Dream." Joe's Big Idea, NPR, December 19, 2017. https://www.youtube.com/watch?v=PSu52CAtpf8.

TRAINING & INSTINCT

Montessori, Maria. *The Discovery of the Child*. Translated by Mary A. Johnstone. Kalakshetra, 1948.

Tallchief, Maria, and Larry Kaplan. *America's Prima Ballerina*. University of Florida Press, 1997.

Sullivan, Kathryn. "Kathryn D. Sullivan." Interview by Jennifer Ross-Nazzal. NASA Johnson Space Center Oral History Project, May 28, 2009. https://www.jsc.nasa.gov/history/oral_histories/SullivanKD/SullivanKD_5-28-09.htm.

Lanier, Cathy. Keynote address. OSAC Women in Security Forum, November 14, 2017.

Fey, Tina. *Bossypants*. Little, Brown, and Company, 2011.

Banghart, Courtney. "The Best Leaders Share Their Journey." Head Coach Training Center, January 16, 2018. http://www.headcoachtc.com/2018/01/16/the-best-leaders-share-their-journey-courtney-banghart.

COURAGE & CAUTION

Barton, Clara. *The Story of My Childhood*. Baker & Taylor, 1907.

Coleman, Bessie. Quoted in *African-American Pioneers in Aviation*. Educational Services, National Air and Space Museum, Smithsonian Institution, 1999.

Mead, Margaret. *And Keep Your Powder Dry: An Anthropologist Looks at America*. W. Morrow, 1943.

Lin, Maya. Artist's statement. The Wave Field, 1998.

Krawcheck, Sallie. "Power Talk." Athena Center for Leadership Studies, Barnard College, February 2015. https://barnard.edu/magazine/spring-2015/career-due-dilligence.

Gbowee, Leymah. Commencement address. Proctor Academy, June 2, 2016.

OVERCOME & BECOME

Wellington, Sheila. "The Voice of Experience." Edited by Lucy McCauley and Christine Canabou. Fast Company, April 30, 2001. https://www.fastcompany.com/42775/voice-experience.

Greenwald, Alice. "We Now Have a Museum That Tells Our 9/11 Story." CBS News, May 15, 2014. https://www.cbsnews.com/news/september-11-memorial-museum-a-museum-that-tells-our-911-story.

DeGeneres, Ellen (@TheEllenShow). Social media post. Twitter, October 2, 2017. https://twitter.com/theellenshow/status/914896502992003072?lang=en.

Duckworth, Tammy. Speech. The Democratic National Convention, Philadelphia, July 28, 2016.

Burke, Tarana (@TaranaBurke). Social media post. Twitter, November 28, 2017.

Swift, Taylor. "Taylor Swift Promises 'Change' on Her Next Record." Interview by Kory Grow. RollingStone, October 15, 2013.

CONVICTION & COMPROMISE

Anthony, Susan B. Speech. National Convention of the Woman's National Loyal League, May 14, 1863.

Faust, Drew Gilpin. "Historians All." Morning Prayers, Harvard University, August 31, 2016.

Figueres, Christiana. "Impossible Isn't a Fact; It's an Attitude." TED2016, Vancouver Convention Center, February 15, 2016.

Williams, Venus. "Venus Williams' Best Business Advice? Say 'No' with a Smile." Article by Christina Austin. Fortune, September 7, 2017. http://fortune.com/2017/09/07/us-open-2017-venus-williams-business-advice.

Gabbard, Tulsi. "Rep. Tulsi Gabbard Rocks the House with Aloha at Sanders Rally in Miami." YouTube, March 13, 2016. https://www.youtube.com/watch?v=Q2f6rdvMBT4.

Lawrence, Jennifer. "Why Do I Make Less Than My Male Co-Stars?" Lenny Letter, October 13, 2015. https://www.lennyletter.com/story/jennifer-lawrence-why-do-i-make-less-than-my-male-costars.

SPEAK UP & LISTEN

Anderson, Marian. My Lord, What a Morning. The Viking Press, 1956.

Albright, Madeleine. Commencement address. Scripps College, May 14, 2016.

Cain, Susan. "Manifesto." The Quiet Revolution. https://www.quietrev.com/manifesto. Accessed April 1, 2018.

Webb, Kinari. Commencement address. Yale Medicine, May 22, 2017. https://healthinharmony.org/2017/06/06/founder-dr-kinari-webb-gives-yale-medicine-commencement-address.

Al-Khatahtbeh, Amani. Panel discussion. The United State of Women Summit, The White House, June 6, 2016.

Gražinytė-Tyla, Mirga. "Politico 28 Class of 2018." Politico. https://www.politico.eu/list/politico-28-2018-ranking/mirga-grazinyte-tyla. Accessed April 1, 2018.

SUBSTANCE & STYLE

Vreeland, Diana. Personal mantra. Quoted in "Diana Vreeland." Profile by Lisa Immordino Vreeland. Harper's Bazaar, August 26, 2011. https://www.harpersbazaar.com/culture/features/a775/diana-vreeland-bazaar-years-0911.

O'Connor, Sandra Day. "Portia's Progress." 23rd James Madison Lecture on Constitutional Law. New York University School of Law, October 29, 1991.

Waters, Alice. Coming to My Senses. PenguinRandomHouse, 2017.

DuVernay, Ava. Keynote speech. The Essence Festival, July 3, 2016.

Clooney, Amal. "Amal Clooney: 'Yazidids in Iraq Are IS Genocide Victims.'" Interview with Fiona Bruce. BBC News at Six, March 7, 2017. www.bbc.co.uk/news/av/world-middle-east-39198623/amal-clooney-yazidis-in-iraq-are-is-genocide-victims.

Wilbur, Matika. "One Woman's Mission to Photograph Every Native American Tribe in the US." Interview by Hilal Isler. The Guardian, September 7, 2015. https://www.theguardian.com/us-news/2015/sep/07/native-american-photographs-matika-wilbur-project-562.

GET IT DONE & UNPLUG

Addams, Jane. "Recreation as a Public Function in Urban Communities." *American Journal of Sociology,* Vol. 17, No. 5 (March 1912).

Tabei, Junko. "No Mountain Too High for Her." *Sports Illustrated*, April 29, 1996.

Slaughter, Anne-Marie. Commencement address. University of Utah, May 6, 2016.

Gilbert, Elizabeth. *Eat, Pray, Love*. Penguin, 2006.

Rudolph, Maya. "Natasha Lyonne." *Interview Magazine*, June 4, 2014. https://www.interviewmagazine.com/culture/natasha-lyonne-1.

Benzakein, Erin. "Creative and Analytical." *Heroine podcast*, November 9, 2017. http://www.heroine.fm.

PLEASE & THANK YOU

Queen Elizabeth II. "Remarks on the 70th Anniversary of D-Day." State banquet, Élysée Palace, Paris, June 6, 2014.

Walker, Alice. "Alice Walker Calls God 'Mama.'" Interview by BeliefNet, February 2007. http://www.beliefnet.com/wellness/2007/02/alice-walker-calls-god-mama.aspx?.

Strode, Muriel. "Wind-Wafted Wild Flowers." The Open Court, Vol. 17, No. 8 (August 1903).

"The true measure of all our actions is how long the good in them lasts."

QUEEN ELIZABETH II
MONARCH

PLEASE & THANK YOU

" 'Thank you' is the best prayer that anyone could say. I say that one a lot. 'Thank you' expresses extreme gratitude, humility, understanding."

ALICE WALKER
NOVELIST

To those around us who listen & laugh, advise
& revise, challenge & champion, design & develop,
fact-check & finesse, open doors & inspire . . .
we see you. We're beyond grateful.

PAULINE'S & ALICIA'S FAMILY & MUSES
Roger Weger • Shawn Weger • Lexi Weger • Rich, Beata & Rosie Renehan • Kathleen, Bill & Jen •
Peter Riley • Rosa Riley • Wendy Williamson • Peter Williamson • Claudia Riley

UNWAVERING BELIEVERS
Sharon Bertschi • Tammy Williams • Sally Browne • Shirley Kappa • Dave Kent • Emily Williams •
Courtney Ferrell • Mason New

ANGELS & ADVISORS
Donna Morea • Ken Bartee • Sharon Schaaf • Lisa Mascolo • Justin & Deb Dunie • Linda Kent •
Megan Beyer • Bill Tyler

PUBLISHING & DESIGN PROS
Rage Kindelsperger • Keyla Hernández • Philip Buchanan • Merideth Harte • Lydia Rasmussen •
Cara Donaldson • Nicole Schiele • Lorina Lana • John Groton• John Foster

COLLABORATORS & BRAINSTORMERS
A shout-out to Girl Scouts Nation's Capital for allowing us to tap your thinking while researching quoteurs.
We're fans {and former Scouts} who admire the Girls Scouts' rich tradition of developing future leaders.
Thank you, Lidia Soto-Harmon • Betsy Thurston • Nancy Wood • Kathy Albarado • Eri Guthrie {Girl Scout}

Cheers!
Pauline & Alicia

About the Authors

Pauline Weger

STORYTELLER • CITESEER • SOCIAL ENTREPRENEUR

Pauline loves discovering creative ways to share inspiring ideas and true stories of real women and girls.

She believes the world is filled with great female role models—you just need to know where to find them. It's why she founded Quotabelle.

Grit & Grace is Pauline's third book. Her writings have appeared in the *Washington Post,* and she has been featured in the Sunday *Washington Post Magazine* and on *NPR* and *Voice of America*.

Pauline grew up in Manchester-by-the-Sea, a small coastal town north of Boston. She and her husband now live in northern Virginia. Mom to two daughters, she stepped away from the corporate world to spend her days creatively bringing balance to the world.

Alicia Williamson

STORYTELLER • CITESEER • CHIEF EDITOR

Alicia Williamson is an author-activist and feminist educator who loves to use her keyboard for good. Since earning her PhD in Literature and Women Studies, she has served as a university lecturer, community organizer, and chief editor.

Whatever the context or medium, Alicia's work is dedicated to amplifying underrepresented voices. She's delighted to be finding engaging new ways to do just that as part of the core team at Quotabelle. Her writings have been published by Wiley, Cambridge University Press, and Quarto. *Grit & Grace* is Alicia's third book written for Quotabelle.

Originally from the Lake Country of northern Minnesota, she now resides in the UK with her husband and their baby daughter.

"I will not follow where the path may lead, but I will go where there is no path, and I will leave a trail."

MURIEL STRODE
AUTHOR

QUOTABELLE

We discover the ideas and stories of real women & girls.
And make them shareable.

To spark innovation. To create connections.
To bring balance to the world.